JANE'S NAVAL REVIEW

edited by Captain John Moore RN

JANE'S NAVAL REVIEW

edited by Captain John Moore RN

Fifth year of issue

JANE'S

Copyright © Jane's Publishing Ltd 1986

First published in the United Kingdom in 1986 by
Jane's Publishing Company Limited
238 City Road, London EC1V 2PU

Distributed in the Philippines and the
USA and its dependencies by
Jane's Publishing Inc
115 Fifth Avenue
New York, NY 10003

ISBN 0 7106 0370 3

Printed and bound in Great Britain by
Biddles Ltd, Guildford and King's Lynn

Contents

The contributors   7

The naval year   9
by Desmond Wettern

Naval aviation and the resurgence of the aircraft carrier   17
by Paul Beaver

Soviet submarine propulsion: signs of a great leap forward?   28
by Cdr Roy Corlett RN

France's commitment to a nuclear navy   36
by Ingénieur en Chef de l'Armement Tournyol du Clos

Soviet Navy: the king is dead . . .   42
by Yossef Bodansky

US Navy: full speed ahead . . . but what course?   47
by Vice-Adm M. S. Holcomb USN

Budget pressures threaten British amphibious fleet   62
by Joseph Porter

The Indian Ocean's uneasy rim   70
by Capt John Moore RN

Torpedoes for tomorrow   84
by Cdr Roy Corlett RN

Ruling the airwaves: electronic warfare at sea   97
by Martin Streetly

Anti-mine hovercraft: has their time come?   107
by G. H. Elsey

AEGIS shoots down the critics   114
by Adm James D. Watkins USN

NATO's naval problems: severe but surmountable   120
by Dr J. M. Luns

Latin American navies: living beyond their means   126
by Adrian English

South-east Asia: a key alliance under pressure   137
by Capt John Moore RN

US Ready Reserve Force: lifeboats for a nation   144
by Nigel Ling

Who shall defend the Canadian Arctic?   151
by John D. Harbron

Rising stakes in the Northern Waters   157
by Clive Archer and David Scrivener

Navies in a terrorist world   166
by Prof Paul Wilkinson

Editor's note

The aim of this book is to provide up-to-date commentaries on maritime affairs. In certain cases the rapid turn of events has rendered these contributions out of date before they even reached the editor's desk. As a result, changes and cancellations have been frequent. If it had not been for the patience and industry of Brendan Gallagher at Jane's, this *Review* would have been further delayed. I am greatly indebted to a good friend and a tireless editor for all that he has done.

John Moore

The Contributors

Archer, Dr Clive, and Scrivener, David

Members of the Department of Politics and International Relations, Aberdeen University. Joint authors/editors of a new book on the problems of Arctic strategy, due for publication in October 1986 and source of the article in this *Review*.

Beaver, Paul

Has been writing about naval aviation, with particular emphasis on aircraft carriers, for nearly 12 years. He is author of *The British Carrier*, a standard work on the Royal Navy's conventional aircraft carriers, and *Invincible Class*, which details the development of the current British light carriers. Since 1982 he has been the editor of *Defence Helicopter World*, the world's only international magazine specialising in military helicopters.

Bodansky, Yossef

Consultant on Soviet affairs to the US State Department and the Pentagon, and a regular contributor to *Jane's Defence Weekly*.

Corlett, Commander Roy, RN

Joined RN 1937 as an artificer and subsequently served in HM Submarines in all rates and ranks up to commander. Final appointment as Staff Weapons Officer to Flag Officer Submarines. Retired at own request and worked with Vickers Shipbuilding Ltd until becoming naval consultant. Adviser and contributor *Jane's Fighting Ships*, *Jane's Defence Review* and a number of technical magazines.

English, Adrian

Born in 1939, he has been interested in the Latin American military scene for many years. He has visited most of the countries of the region and is an internationally acknowledged expert on Latin American military affairs. Since 1979 he has annually contributed material to *Jane's Fighting Ships* and *The Military Balance*. He has also written extensively on Latin American military and strategic subjects, including regular contributions to *Jane's Defence Review*, *Jane's Defence Weekly*, *International Defence Review*, *Navy International* and *Technologia Militar*, and was co-author of *Battle for the Falklands: Naval Forces*.

Harbron, Commander John D., RCN(R)(Retd)

Foreign affairs and defence analyst for Thomson Newspapers in Canada and a frequent contributor on naval topics to US, British and Canadian publications. Among his areas of special interest are icebreakers, Soviet and European Arctic shipping, and Canadian naval affairs.

Holcomb, Vice-Adm M. S., USN(Retd)

Retired from the US Navy in May 1985 after 36 years of service. His last assignment was as Deputy CINCUSNAVEUR and US Commander Eastern Atlantic, headquartered in London. Earlier appointments included command of the US 7th Fleet and Carrier Group 1. A naval aviator, he specialised in carrier-based anti-submarine warfare as a pilot, squadron commander and CO of the interim sea control ship USS *Guam*. He is now a consultant in national security matters, based in Washington DC.

Ling, Nigel, TEng(CEI)

Served as a Merchant Navy engineer officer, worked on research and development of fishing vessels, including stability investigations, and is currently with the British Transport Docks Board, concerned with naval architecture and design.

Luns, Dr J. M. A. H.

Former Secretary-General of NATO, first appointed in 1971. Achieved the rank of Leading Signalman in the Royal Netherlands Navy during his national service. Served with Netherlands Ministry for Foreign Affairs from 1938 until 1952, and as Minister for Foreign Affairs 1952–1971.

Moore, Captain J. E., RN

Entered RN 1939. Served most of naval career in HM Submarines. Commanded 7th Submarine Squadron, was Chief of Staff to Commander-in-Chief Naval Home Command and, finally, took charge of Soviet naval intelligence in MoD. Retired at own request 1972. Editor *Jane's Fighting Ships* since November 1972. Author of several books and numbers of articles on naval affairs.

Porter, Joseph

A distinguished commentator on naval affairs who has taken a keen interest in amphibious warfare.

Streetly, Martin

Freelance writer and illustrator specialising in airborne electronic warfare. His books include *Confound and Destroy*, a history of the RAF's wartime bomber support group, and *World Electronic Warfare Aircraft*. He is a regular contributor to *Jane's Defence Weekly*.

Watkins, Adm James

US Navy Chief of Naval Operations, following appointments as Vice-Chief and of Naval Operations and Chief of Naval Personnel. Was one of the US Navy's early nuclear submarine captains.

Wettern, Desmond

Served in the RNVR, RN and RNR from 1950 to 1970. Appointed naval correspondent of the *Sunday Telegraph* in 1961 and of the *Daily Telegraph* in 1972. Books include *The Lonely Battle* (1960) and *The Decline of British Sea Power* (1982). Founder and council member of the British Maritime League.

Wilkinson, Prof Paul

Professor of International Relations and head of the Department of Politics and International Relations at Aberdeen University, he has studied the phenomenon of terrorism for the past 20 years. Other works include *Political Terrorism* (published 1974) and *Terrorism and the Liberal State* (1977, new edition 1986).

The naval year

Desmond Wettern

The past year has seen three developments that signal profound and long-term changes in naval strategy which will no doubt spill over into the tactical field. Late in 1985 it became known that Admiral Sergei Gorshkov had at last been replaced as Commander-in-Chief of the Soviet Navy by Admiral Vladimir Chernavin. Also towards the end of last year, the US Assistant Secretary of the Navy, Melvyn Paisley, disclosed that in some areas of submarine design the Soviet Navy had now established a lead and was not relying as heavily as had been widely supposed on technology bought or stolen from the West. At the beginning of this year Admiral James D. Watkins, USN Chief of Naval Operations, spelled out in a lengthy essay the facts of current American maritime strategy.

There have been other developments of long-term significance, such as the French decision to go ahead with a new generation of nuclear-powered conventional aircraft carriers, which will have an impact on the global maritime scene of the future. But, except perhaps in the case of Britain among the larger naval powers, the acquisition of new ships and equipment is dictated by the requirements of national political strategy.

Soviet Alfa-class attack submarine. Last year saw an admission by Assistant Secretary of the US Navy Melvyn Paisley that the Soviet Union had established a lead over the West in some areas of submarine technology. (*G. Jacobs*)

Gorshkov, who held the Soviet Navy's supreme appointment for almost 30 years and was also a Deputy Defence Minister, presided over the rise of the Red Fleet from a coast defence force to a point where it has a global potential. He emphasised the importance of a balanced fleet and in his writings claimed that the failure of the Nazi U-boats was due to an almost total lack of co-ordination with the surface fleet and the Luftwaffe. As the oceanic capability of the Soviet Navy grew, he put forward the novel, by Russian standards, view that the fleet was capable of independent operations by virtue of its mobility far beyond the waters surrounding the homeland. He wrote of its important contribution to the land battle, with its ability to take the war to an enemy across the seas.

Chernavin – who before becoming Chief of the Main Naval Staff in Moscow had commanded the Northern Fleet, in which the bulk of Soviet strategic ballistic missile submarines are concentrated – at least once publicly contradicted this view, underlining the interdependence of all arms of the armed forces within an overall strategic policy laid down by the Communist Party. That Chernavin should hold such an opinion, having had command of a large slice of the Soviet nuclear deterrent, is hardly surprising. He also appears to embrace the traditional Russian strategy of concentration of force. Gorshkov, on the other hand, appeared to advocate the "first strike" philosophy, under which the Russian naval forces around the globe would strike first in war to gain the advantage of surprise.

Under Gorshkov the Soviet Navy's greatest progress has been in the build-up of a modern submarine fleet. In this alone there was nothing very revolutionary: it is too often forgotten that as far back as the beginning of the Second World War Russia boasted the world's largest submarine fleet. As a submariner himself, Chernavin may be expected to continue this emphasis.

Much more significant will be any move Chernavin chooses to make to remedy the serious gaps in the Soviet Navy's order of battle left by his predecessor. In September 1981, when still C-in-C of the Northern Fleet, he had operational control of ZAPAD-81, the largest amphibious exercise ever mounted by the Russian Navy. Although it was staged in the Baltic, many of the amphibious and other ships involved came from the Northern Fleet. Such was the Russians' sensitivity over the exercise that the destroyer HMS *Glasgow* suffered minor damage in a collision with a Soviet warship while keeping close watch on ships departing from their Kola Peninsula bases.

ZAPAD-81 was conducted under the umbrella of shore-based air support and no great distances or long ocean passages were involved. Thus the lack of both air support and the amphibious forces needed in areas far beyond the Russian shores, particularly for an opposed landing, must be something of which Chernavin will be very well aware. Whether the new nuclear-powered carriers – the first of which should be at sea by around 1990 – will be used to remedy the lack of air support for amphibious forces outside Soviet-controlled waters remains to be seen. But if

Chernavin intends to complete the task of creating a fully oceanic fleet, much will depend on his success in obtaining funds and political approval for more long-range amphibious ships like the *Ivan Rogov* and *Aleksandr Nikolaev* and the dry stores replenishment ships and tankers that would be essential to distant expeditions in any strength. Judging by the number of possibly prototype designs of new nuclear-powered attack submarines that have been completed in the last couple of years, it may well be that the expansion of the surface fleet's capabilities will have to wait until the way forward for the submarine fleet is clearer. But divination of Soviet naval policy is always a chancy business, as, for example, in the case of the completion in 1980–81 of the first two specially designed hospital ships, *Ob* and *Yenisei*. This was seen by some in the West as indicating that the Russians were contemplating direct involvement in military adventures in the Third World. In fact it appears that one of the ships is used primarily to boost the morale of Cuban surrogates in places like Angola by providing some measure of sophisticated medical support for the sick and wounded.

While evidence, or the lack of it, of a build-up of Russian amphibious and logistic support forces may give some indication of Chernavin's plans for the future of the surface fleet outside home waters, there can be little doubt that the submarine fleet will continue to enjoy the degree of priority that in 1985 prompted the former US Director of Naval Intelligence, Rear-Admiral John Butts, to tell Congress that "over the past five years the Soviets have launched an unprecedented number and variety of nuclear attack submarines". The balance in Russian shipyards appeared to have shifted in their favour at the expense of ballistic missile submarines. "We believe this construction programme" is primarily to "close the technological gap between Soviet and Western

---

The **Mike class** is amongst a flood of new nuclear-powered attack submarine designs to have emerged from Soviet yards within the last couple of years.

The British *Trafalgar*-class attack submarines are reckoned to be amongst the quietest in the world, surpassing even the best conventional boats. The US Navy ascribes this to the use of shrouded propulsors.

submarines. Since the introduction of the Victor III-class SSN (in 1978), the Soviets have steadily reduced the technological inferiority of their newest submarines".

Assistant Secretary Paisley went further still in declaring in a partially classified statement that in some submarine technologies the Russians were ahead of the US. He cited "quieting, strengthened double hulls, higher speed, higher reserve buoyancy and deeper operations" as advances which were by and large not stolen or bought from the West. In technologies such as "high-power-density material and high-strength hull material (presumably a reference to the titanium used in the hulls of the Alfa and probably the succeeding Mike-class SSNs) . . . the Soviets are ahead of the US. . . ."

This lead has been admitted by personnel working on the US Navy's SSN-21 *Seawolf* programme, the first boat of which is due to be ordered in Fiscal Year 1989. They say that it will probably not match the Alfa class for speed. But the US submarines will enjoy the classic advantage of being quieter, not least because of their shrouded propulsors, which, the Americans say, the Royal Navy already has at sea. It is

probably this system that has in the main made the latest British SSNs, the *Trafalgar* class, quieter than even the *Oberon*-class diesel-electric submarines, believed to be among the quietest in the world.

It has been pointed out by men like Admiral Wesley L. McDonald USN, before he retired last year from his appointment as Supreme Allied Commander Atlantic, that in order to attack a convoy or task group a submarine would have to remain as quiet as possible, and that high speed (with a consequent major increase in noise) would be of value only for escaping after launching an attack. But high speed could certainly be of value to a submarine moving from its base to its operational area, though again this would increase the risk of detection by systems such as the Sound Surveillance Systems (SOSUS) laid in certain key areas on the seabed.

Clearly, Western anti-submarine sensors and weapons will have to take into account the increasing speed, hull strength and diving depth of Soviet submarines. In thus giving some of their submarines a measure of immunity to some Western countermeasures the Russians have solved part of the equation. The danger for the West lies in their ability to solve the other part by making noise reductions comparable to that of the British *Trafalgar* class. In this respect the activities of the "Walker family" of spies in America and some naval attachés at the Soviet Embassy in London in the past few years must be a cause for profound concern.

It is ironic that the Russians should be ahead in designing submarines to defeat enemy countermeasures with higher speeds and greater diving depths, since their SSNs' primary task, judging by their infrequent exercising in convoy attacks and interdiction of seaborne lines of communication, appears to be defence of their own ballistic missile submarines (SSBN). This task calls for quiet-running boats able to lie stopped for long periods making minimal noise, rather than for high-speed pursuits.

According to Admiral Watkins, in his essay "The Maritime Strategy", the prime task of the NATO navies must be to take the initiative at a time of crisis and at the start of a conflict with the Soviet Union. To achieve this he calls for a strategy of forward deploy-ment to try to nip crises in the bud before they can escalate into full-scale war. But if war should come, it would be the task of Allied forces to seek out those of the enemy around the globe to prevent the Soviets from concentrating their efforts in a single theatre. To safeguard the Atlantic convoys carrying reinforcements to Western Europe – and to avoid a repeat of 1942, when just 14 of Nazi Germany's 50 operational U-boats sank 450 Allied ships in the first seven months of the year – he sees the NATO carrier battle groups moving forward to "wage an aggressive campaign against all Soviet submarines including ballistic missile

In the event of full-scale war, NATO carrier battle groups would campaign aggressively against Soviet submarines of all types. Heart of each battle group would be a US Navy fleet carrier, with a British *Invincible*-class light carrier giving defensive anti-submarine support. Seen here in company with USS *Ranger* (middle) are HMS *Invincible* (foreground) and the frigate HMS *Rothesay*. *(Royal Navy)*

submarines". He also sees it as "essential to conduct forward operations with attack submarines, as well as to establish barriers at key world chokepoints using maritime patrol aircraft, mines, attack submarines, or sonobuoys, to prevent leakage of enemy forces to the open ocean where the Western Alliance's resupply lines can be threatened".

The idea of attacking Soviet ballistic missile submarines has been criticised by some in the US Congress and elsewhere as a recipe for immediate escalation of the conflict by Moscow. "But", Admiral Watkins points out, "escalation solely as a result of actions at sea seems improbable, given the Soviet land orientation. Escalation in response to maritime pressure serves no useful purpose for the Soviets since their reserve forces would be degraded and the United States' retaliatory posture would be enhanced. Neither we nor the Soviets can rule out the possibility that escalation will occur, but aggressive use of maritime power can make escalation a less attractive option to the Soviets with the passing of every day."

He goes on to point out that the real issue is not how maritime strategy is influenced by nuclear weapons, but rather how it influences the nuclear equation. As the maritime campaign by the West progressed, so use of nuclear weapons would become less attractive to the Soviets, since the West's ability to maintain the initiative at sea would mean failure for Russian efforts

to decouple Western Europe from North America. Admiral Watkins accepts that this Western strategy is not without risk, and that it does depend upon an early political response to a crisis and the will to take difficult decisions.

When, in autumn last year, NATO carrier task groups penetrated deep into the Norwegian Sea during exercises, this manifestation of the forward strategy was hailed by some sections of the media as something new. But it was really a return to a strategy which has held sway for many years but which has recently been hampered by lack of resources, in the deployment of surface forces at least. The return to a forward strategy by NATO owes much to the promptings of men like Admiral of the Fleet Sir John Fieldhouse during his time as Allied C-in-C Channel and Eastern Atlantic. As a submariner he saw that Western SSNs, given the huge numerical balance in the Russians' favour, should operate in peacetime in those waters where in war they would be seeking out Soviet forces before they could gain entry to the deep oceans.

In February this year the forward strategy was given a further boost by President Reagan, who pointed out that the Soviet Navy and air forces occupied positions from which they could dominate many of the 16 chokepoints vital for the movement of Free World shipping. Clearly, the West could not afford to let these passages be seized by Soviet forces and must be in a position to take the initiative in order to secure them.

Focus on the chokepoints also serves to show the relevance of navies other than those of the United States and Soviet Union to the control of what are likely to be the focal points for confrontation, whether directly between the two superpowers or between their allies and surrogates. Four of the passages enumerated by President Reagan – the Skaggerak,

Kattegat, the Greenland-Iceland-UK (GIUK) line and the Straits of Gibraltar – lie within the NATO area, while the Suez Canal approaches, the Florida Strait and the Panama Canal approaches are peripheral to it.

Taking the first two, the continuing failure of the Danes to acquire the NATO Link 11 for automatic data transmission means that while Federal German Navy (FGN) fast attack craft (FAC) in the Baltic can co-ordinate their tactics with American carriers and their aircraft operating in the North Sea on the other side of the Jutland peninsula, communications with Danish FACs and their command organisation still rely primarily on easily jammed voice circuits. The Danes' stopgap purchase of three submarines from Norway and development of the Flex 300 design as a cheaper means of replacing a number of their minor war vessels are to be welcomed, but close co-ordination with the FGN would seem to be more in the long-term NATO interest.

The GIUK line would initially be a prime Royal Navy responsibility. Increasing the number of Sea Harriers from five to, eventually, 12 in each of the two operational *Invincible*-class carriers should greatly improve the air defence capability of the ships maintaining the line until US carrier air support is available. Two carriers will be the minimum, but the availability of even these will depend upon ending the nonsense of using an *Invincible* as an amphibious carrier to take British and Netherlands commandos to Norway as the spearhead of Allied reinforcements of

HMS *Fearless*, one of the Royal Navy's two amphibious assault ships. The demands of Northern Flank reinforcement suggest that their successors – if they are ever ordered – should have significant hangar capacity. (*Royal Navy*)

NATO's northern flank. If for no other reason, the problems of maintaining numbers of helicopters on the hangar-less flight decks of the assault ships *Fearless* and *Intrepid* in temperatures far below zero should dictate the provision of a ship with a "through deck" (i.e. hangar) capability as a matter of urgency. This is made all the more necessary by the Government's determination to sell the carrier *Hermes*, which had the capacity to embark a commando, its vehicles and helicopters, and four landing craft while maintaining a force of Sea Harriers and ASW helicopters on board. The premature scrapping of the heavy repair ship *Triumph*, a former carrier, a few weeks before the start of the Falklands War, in which she would have played a vital role, underlined the need for the retention of at least one large warship in mothballs at all times to meet contingencies. As a piece of diplomacy, the sale of *Hermes* to India, which may have become a reality by the time these words are published, will hardly lessen Indian dependence upon the Soviet Union for naval equipment. With the Russians now apparently demanding an economic market rate for the warships it supplies, the honeymoon between Moscow and New Delhi, if not the marriage itself, may be ending anyway.

But British maritime policy, military and civil, appears to be dictated not by what is required for the security of an island nation still dependent for its survival on seaborne trade but by the amount of money that can be spared after paying for a host of other demands upon the national income that have little or no relevance to security. These include the enormous administrative and welfare "tail" of the forces in Germany, and the retention of a highly costly strategic nuclear capability in the form of Trident, for which no real alternative, such as Tomahawk cruise missile, has ever been fully considered.

The fourth chokepoint in the NATO area, the Straits of Gibraltar, would also initially be a British responsibility, currently discharged by deploying a guardship at or near the Rock. Clearly, any serious attempt by Moscow either to force a passage by its Mediterranean squadron into the Atlantic or to reinforce that squadron from elsewhere would have to be countered by the American Sixth Fleet.

The Americans would also be exclusively responsible for the safety of the Suez Canal, the approaches to the Panama Canal and the Straits of Florida, where the Cuban Navy's 32 missile and torpedo-armed fast attack craft, three submarines and the air force could represent a significant threat to Allied transatlantic reinforcement shipping.

While America could look to friendly nations such as Egypt, Oman, Britain and France for assistance in the defence of Suez, Bab al Mandab at the southern end of the Red Sea, and Hormuz at the entrance to the Gulf, her Indian Ocean carrier task group would play

HMS *Hermes*: will this Falklands veteran end her days as flagship of the Indian Navy? (*C. & S. Taylor*)

Cuba's trio of Foxtrot patrol submarines would represent a worrying hazard for Allied reinforcement shipping.

a vital role in the defence of the second and third. But France periodically deploys one of her two existing carriers to reinforce her reasonably substantial Indian Ocean squadron, something that might well be increased in the 1990s, given the greater endurance of projected nuclear-powered replacements for *Clemenceau* and *Foch*. Moreover, the French might well feel less constrained by political considerations than the Americans if any attempt was made by Soviet surrogates, perhaps in South Yemen, to interdict one of these waterways.

It could well be that the French might be more acceptable than any other Western nation if help were needed in the event of a threat to the Cape of Good Hope chokepoint, an area of a growing power vacuum as the South African Navy's oceangoing ships and its maritime patrol aircraft age or are withdrawn and

national policy dictates coastal defence rather than an oceanic role.

While the ASEAN nations would initially be responsible for security of the Malacca and Sunda straits and the Philippines for that of the Makassar Strait, any serious threat from the Soviet naval and air forces at Cam Ranh Bay in Vietnam would have to be countered by the US Seventh Fleet. Retention of the USN base at Subic Bay in the Philippines is therefore vital, even though the Americans could rightly expect assistance from Australia and Japan, much of whose trade passes through these waterways. Japan and South Korea would also have a role to play in the defence of the Tsushima or Korea Strait.

The extent of American naval responsibilities in the Pacific is immense, extending from Indonesia to the Gulf of Alaska, through which passes more oil for the American consumer than is brought from Saudi Arabia, and from the Yellow Sea in the west to the coast of California in the east.

Last of President Reagan's 16 chokepoints is the Magellan Strait, where Britain, alone among America's allies, maintains a naval presence close by. The Falklands' value as a base for Western naval operations in the event of a global conflict has been conceded by Navy Secretary Lehman, but the strategic position the Royal Navy now occupies in the South Atlantic would appear to have escaped the notice of British politicians

busy counting the cost of the island's garrison – possibly because the Soviet Navy has not so far operated in the area. British Parliamentarians also seem to be unaware of the fact that with their huge fishing fleet the Russians are building up experience of operating in this area, given the number of both active and reserve naval personnel to be found among the crews of these ships.

Expenditure on the security of the Falklands is in fact seen as a total loss on the economic balance sheet. While ships returning home from a stint around the Falklands do often call at a South American port on the way, such visits are in the nature of rest and

France's pair of highly capable fleet carriers and independent stance make her the obvious Western flag-bearer in the event of Middle Eastern contingencies. The French Navy's freedom of action will be further increased in the 1990s when *Clemenceau* (pictured here) and *Foch* are replaced by their nuclear-powered successors. (*ECPA*)

Leander-class frigate *Almirante Lynch* of the Chilean Navy. Valuable sales of naval material to Chile, Argentina and Brazil resulted from the Royal Navy's regular goodwill visits to South American countries during the 1960s. (*C. & S. Taylor*)

recreation. It is thus doubtful whether they are seen in Whitehall as a means of fostering overseas sales of British goods, as the periodic South American cruises by RN squadrons in the 1960s did so well. Such deployments led to sales of *Leander*-class frigates and *Oberon*-class submarines to Chile, Vosper Thornycroft-designed frigates and more *Oberon*s to Brazil, and Type 42 destroyers to Argentina. But then the permanent, albeit small, Royal Navy presence in the area withered away until the events of 1982. Could this also explain why, despite a number of task group deployments, sales of new British warship designs in the Far East have been negligible since the final withdrawal of a permanent naval presence (apart from the Hong Kong local squadron) in the early 1970s? Is there a link, too, between the retention by France of a credible Indian Ocean squadron and the sale in 1980 to Saudi Arabia, in the face of intense British and US competition, of four frigates and two replenishment ships in a £1,400 million deal, the largest of its kind to involve any Western nation in recent years?

The United States is making steady progress towards the creation of its 600-ship Navy. France plans two new carriers, the first in the West outside the US to be nuclear-powered, and continues to build ballistic missile submarines. Russia is challenging Western technology in the field of undersea warfare. And China has an ambitious programme of naval expansion, with new SSNs, destroyers, frigates and mine countermeasures vessels. In 1986 Britain will complete one frigate but will pay off three and a destroyer, and is having great problems finding the money to order three frigates on which work should have begun last year. Yet in February this year Admiral Sir William Staveley, the First Sea Lord, saw no way of cutting the Royal Navy's commitments. He gave no clue as to how the resources were to be found to match them, only assuring his audience that the service was in "good heart". Why this should be, with no apparent end to the process of maritime retrenchment, he did not explain.

Naval aviation and the resurgence of the aircraft carrier

Paul Beaver

Defending the USN's aircraft carriers and their supporting task groups, the Grumman F-14 Tomcat is a remarkable aircraft with the ability to track multiple targets and engage at least six simultaneously using the Phoenix stand-off air-defence missile. (*Grumman*)

In the 1970s it was generally assumed that the aircraft carrier had passed the mantle of capital ship of the world's major navies to the nuclear-powered submarine. This had a sobering effect on naval aviation, despite the increased use of helicopters aboard surface escorts. Since 1980, however, there have been a number of developments which suggest a swing back towards the conventional fixed-wing aircraft carrier. At the same time, smaller, non-conventional designs are proving attractive to many nations with a limited budget.

In peacetime the aircraft carrier remains an ideal instrument of foreign policy, as demonstrated by the recent deployments of American carriers in the Mediterranean, Indian Ocean and Caribbean, and by the Soviet decision to build a class of nuclear-powered ships, their first true fleet carriers. France and Argentina are also set to keep big carriers in their fleets until the turn of the century and beyond. But it is the advent of the light carrier operating short take-off and vertical landing (STOVL) aircraft that is having the most obvious effect on naval aviation. This combination has allowed Britain, India, Spain and, probably, Italy to stay in the carrier business on a reduced budget. In early 1986 India began negotiating to acquire a third batch of British Aerospace Sea Harrier STOVL fighters, giving a potential strength of 30 aircraft and therefore the ability to form two air groups. This suggests that a second aircraft carrier will be acquired by 1990 to supplement *Vikrant*, which has recently been refitted in a local yard.

India has also been buying large numbers of well equipped medium ASW helicopters from Westland. The latest order covers Sea Kings with the MEL Super Searcher radar and the ability to launch the British Aerospace Sea Eagle anti-shipping missile, which has yet to enter service with the Royal Navy and Royal Air Force. A boosted version of the missile is being developed for the Indian Navy and it is thought that Sea Kings carrying the system will be embarked in *Vikrant* by 1989. In addition, it seems possible that India will seek to buy Thorn EMI Electronics Searchwater radar for a flight of AEW helicopters embarked in the carrier. Such equipment will make the Indian Navy, centred on one or two aircraft carriers, the most effective in the Indian Ocean.

Despite the paying-off and virtual destruction of the Royal Australian Navy's Fleet Air Arm, the carrier club could be expanding once more. Financially straitened Chile has a continuing requirement for a light fleet carrier and has expressed interest in the decommissioned HMS *Hermes*, previously offered to Australia and, more recently, India. But it is the Soviet Union's determination to acquire big decks, complete with steam catapults and arrester gear, that has reawakened the world's navies to the capabilities of the carrier.

Principe de Asturias and other light carriers like her represent a significant fixed-wing naval aviation capability at a price that can be afforded by second-ranking nations.

The US Navy is justifiably proud of the *Nimitz*-class nuclear-powered aircraft carriers, four of which are in commission and two building at Newport News Shipbuilding & Dry Dock. Able to carry 90 aircraft to sea, the CVN is the core of the NATO Striking Fleet. (*Royal Navy*)

The Soviet Navy's first large-scale attempt at naval aviation was the *Moskva* class. Only the lead ship and *Leningrad*, pictured here, were built, possibly because their usefulness was limited by the turbulence thrown off by the sheer aft face of the superstructure. (*Royal Navy*)

Recent indications from Washington show that the Americans still have high regard for the aircraft carrier. There has even been praise for the British *Invincible* class from Navy Secretary John Lehman, who has described the three ships as "quite capable" and remarked that "it would be nice to have some of them in the United States Navy". But the USN regards the 90,000-ton, nuclear-powered *Nimitz* class as the true shape of naval aviation to come, pointing to comparable developments in the USSR. Through the Service Life Extension Programme (SLEP), which will extend the service life of all USN carriers by at least 10–15 years, the Americans hope to maintain 15 carrier battle groups in commission. The bulk of these are currently earmarked for NATO striking fleet employment, although the Pacific Ocean is now beginning to loom larger in strategic calculations, particularly as the USSR improves bases like Vladivostok in the east and strengthens the Pacific Fleet.

SLEP will enable America's older carriers, such as the *Kitty Hawk* and *John F. Kennedy* classes, to carry a full complement of modern aircraft such as the F-18 Hornet, F-14D Tomcat, S-3B Viking and new anti-submarine helicopters. The last-named programme

has been delayed in Congress over the last few years and the production order for the Sikorsky SH-60F Seahawk, due to replace the SH-3 Sea King, is smaller than originally envisaged. This has meant that the Sea King has received its own SLEP, resulting in a fleet of 125 aircraft with modern systems and components which will last until the turn of the century. The updating of the SH-3 and the provision of money to develop the dipping-sonar version of the SH-60 indicates how seriously the Americans take the inner-zone defence of task groups against current and anticipated Soviet attack submarines.

The last five years have witnessed the continuing build-up of the Soviet Navy into a "blue water" fleet and the launching in 1985 of the first 65,000-ton *Kremlin*-class nuclear-powered aircraft carrier and laying down of a second at the same Black Sea yard. Due to join the four *Kiev*-class vessels in the early 1990s, these ships will operate the Soviet Navy's first embarked conventional aircraft. The Russians will have much to learn, but the expensive decision to build ships more capable than the *Kiev* class indicates that the need for organic air cover has now been completely accepted by the Soviet hierarchy.

The *Kiev* class was the Soviet Union's next step on the road to a full-fledged naval aviation capability. This evolution will culminate in the early 1990s with the entry into service of the nuclear-powered fleet carrier *Kremlin*.

Soviet Naval Aviation continues to operate the dated but effective Kamov Ka-25 and Ka-27 series of helicopters from surface escorts and as ASW/ planeguard helicopters from the ASW cruisers and light aircraft carriers; they will probably also be used aboard the new fleet carriers. The Russians still regard shore-based helicopters like the Mil Mi-4 Hound and Mi-14 Haze as the most cost-effective means of keeping anchorages and the approaches to bases free from intruders, just as the Royal Navy bases a squadron of Sea Kings near the nuclear submarine bases on the River Clyde.

Although Britain's "through-deck cruisers", now known as the *Invincible*-class light anti-submarine aircraft carriers (CVS), were well into construction when the last British conventional carrier, *Ark Royal*, was decommissioned in 1978, there was a general feeling of pessimism about the future of aviation in the Royal Navy. One of the major worries concerned the lack of embarked airborne early warning (AEW) aircraft. Events in the spring of 1982 were to prove those fears justified. Although the 20,000-ton *Invincible* and its flagship, the former light fleet carrier *Hermes*, were able to launch and recover aircraft in weather conditions which would have made a conventional carrier's deck unusable, the greater range and stand-off air combat capability of something like the F-4 Phantom would have made combat air patrols less

hazardous and exhausting. More important still, a conventional carrier would have provided AEW cover and thus might have prevented the loss of *Sheffield* and *Atlantic Conveyor*.

Despite its lack of range and the fact that it is a single-seater, the Sea Harrier proved effective in the South Atlantic and confirmed the need for organic fighter protection. This is particularly true of out-of-area operations but also applies to NATO's anti-submarine warfare groups, centred on the *Invincible* class. Recent exercises like Ocean Safari '85 and Autumn Train '85 have underlined the effectiveness of the newly developed helicopter-mounted AEW capability. On at least one occasion the Sea King AEW2 was able to launch and operate in weather which kept the USN's E-2C Hawkeyes chained to the deck. These exercises also showed that full integration between Sea Harrier and Sea King AEW is possible and that their effectiveness could be further increased by developments such as secure speech and data links. The FRS2 update programme will make more effective use of the Sea Harrier's available internal volume and will cut the currently almost intolerable pilot workload.

The combination of large carrier battle groups and smaller ASW groups seems to cover most eventualities in the NATO theatre. But in an effort to fill any remaining gaps the Royal Navy is almost certain to

Right: *Illustrious*, second of the *Invincible*-class light carriers, returns from the South Atlantic with a full complement of embarked aircraft, including nine Sea Harrier FRS1s, eight Sea Kings and one Wessex HU5. (*HMS Illustrious*)

Left: **The rationale behind the British CVS design was originally the need to take a large number of Sea King ASW helicopters to sea in support of the NATO Striking Fleet. But from the mid-1970s onwards the Sea Harrier STOVL fighter has come to assume at least equal prominence. This example, the personal aircraft of the CO of No 801 Sqn, carries a Sidewinder training round on the wing pylon. (*HMS Invincible*)**

Below left: **HMS *Reliant*, a converted container carrier, is spearheading the Royal Navy's effort to spread aviation capability more widely through the fleet and Royal Fleet Auxiliary. (*Royal Navy*)**

Below: ***Giuseppe Garibaldi*, pride of the Italian Navy – but will she ever embark fixed-wing aircraft?**

integrate fully into its strength the previously merchant Royal Fleet Auxiliary. This will allow ASW helicopters to make more use of the decks of replenishment ships; similar deployments of fighter or AEW units are a more distant prospect.

The Royal Navy, NATO's primary anti-submarine force, has still to confirm the full mission package for EH 101, the helicopter that will replace its Sea Kings and those of the Italian Navy. Although the RN is also committed to a light helicopter, in the form of the Advanced Lynx with a new radar and thermal imaging for long-range target detection and identification, EH 101 will be embarked in ASW frigates as well as operating in squadron strength from the *Invincible*-class carriers. EH 101 is due to enter Royal Navy service in 1995. Until then the medium ASW role will be performed by the Advanced Sea King, with new radar and sonar.

The Italian Navy will operate the EH 101 from the new light aircraft carrier *Giuseppe Garibaldi*, which entered service in 1985, complete with a ski-jump for STOVL operations. Ever since it was announced that the ship would carry such a structure there has been speculation that the Italian Navy would acquire the Sea Harrier despite a 60-year-old ruling giving the Italian Air Force sole rights to the country's fixed-wing military aircraft. But it is possible that Italy won't

prove as committed to the EH 101 as was originally hoped. This has nothing to do with the abortive plan for a European rescue of Britain's Westland helicopter company. Rather, with the state-owned Agusta enjoying design leadership of the NFH 90, the Italian forces look likely to divide their money between EH 101 and this nine-tonne NATO-standard shipboard ASW, surface attack and SAR project. NFH 90 is rivalled by several other designs, including the Sikorsky S-70B Seahawk, which has been sold to the Australian and Spanish navies. Although designed specifically for ASW within the USN, the Seahawk has been marketed well by the world's largest helicopter manufacturer, and it is certain that other navies will buy the type in due course.

Following Spain's entry into NATO, that country is now taking on some of the burden of defending the Atlantic shipping lanes. The commissioning of the light aircraft carrier *Principe de Asturias* is therefore seen as an important contribution to Western naval

Below: **Matador STOVL fighters parked on the deck of the current Spanish aircraft carrier, *Dedalo*. Launched as USS *Wilmington* in 1943, she will be replaced by *Principe de Asturias* in 1987.**

Bottom: ***Dedalo* also embarks a wide range of helicopters, including Sea Kings and Bell 212s. (*Aldo Fraccaroli*)**

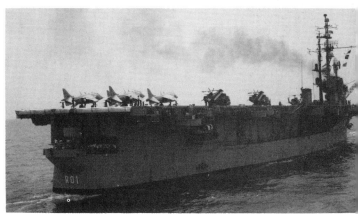

power. In addition, Thorn EMI Electronics has begun delivering Searchwater radar sets which will enable a number of Spanish Navy SH-3 Sea Kings to provide organic AEW. Italy and perhaps India have also expressed interest in the system, while France has a requirement for fixed-wing AEW.

The French Navy has operated conventional fixed-wing aircraft carriers since the end of the Second World War, more recently at the expense of other units in the French fleet. The present pair of carriers, *Foch* and *Clemenceau*, were commissioned in the early 1960s and have subsequently been refitted to operate a new "half-generation" of fighter, the Super Etendard. This aircraft successfully launched Exocet missiles against the British task force off the Falklands and against tankers in the Gulf, and in 1983 over the Lebanon carried the Aéronavale into action for the first time since the Algerian War. In that conflict, and in Indo-China and at Suez, the French used aircraft carriers as instruments of foreign policy and an effective means of projecting air power ashore.

Despite the austerity measures of President Mitterand, the French Navy is planning to build one and possibly two nuclear-powered aircraft carriers to replace *Clemenceau* and *Foch* in the 1990s. Preliminary work on *Richelieu* began in 1984, when long-lead

items were ordered for Brest Naval Dockyard. Apart from the propulsion system, the design is conventional, with an 8.5° angled deck, steam catapults, two aircraft lifts and an air group which will include the Super Etendard and possibly a new AEW aircraft. The latter was expected to have been the US-designed Hawkeye, but recent reports indicate that the French Air Force could be tasked with providing support by means of long-range land-based aircraft; the use of a helicopter has been ruled out.

Although it did not take part in the Falklands War, the Argentinian aircraft carrier *Veinticinco de Mayo* represented a significant threat to the British naval forces in the South Atlantic. A major refit in 1980–81 and subsequent additional work have modernised the ship and greatly improved its fighting ability, not least by permitting her to embark the Super Etendard. In addition, the ship can operate the Grumman S-2E Tracker (widely used aboard the former British *Colossus*-class light fleet carriers, including Brazil's *Minas Gerais* and Australia's now defunct *Melbourne*) and a mix of anti-submarine and amphibious assault helicopters, including the ubiquitous SH-3 Sea King.

This carrier is however now over 40 years old, and it is obvious that the Argentinian Navy would like a replacement. Leading candidate is a STOVL carrier

Above: **One of the French Navy's two current aircraft carriers is *Clemenceau* (flight deck code U), seen operating in the Mediterranean in 1981 with some of the first Super Etendard fighters embarked. Visible on the angled deck area is a Super Frelon anti-submarine helicopter. (*ECPA*)**

Right: **The strike element aboard French aircraft carriers comprises F-8(FN) Crusaders for air defence and Super Etendards for strike and reconnaissance. Here a Crusader is launched past a Super Etendard. (*ECPA*)**

Veinticinco de Mayo, flagship of the Argentinian Navy. (*Dr Robert Scheina*)

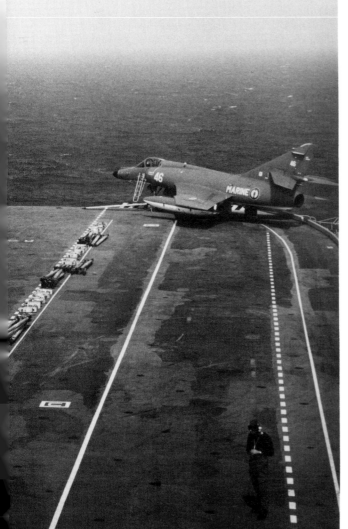

similar to those which will shortly join the navies of Italy and Spain. Cultural and language links make it more probable that the Spanish *Principe de Asturias* design would be favoured, and it has been reported that a enlarged version has been considered. But besides being a funding problem for a navy already considering the sale of some of its larger escorts to foreign buyers, any decision to acquire such a carrier would create a conundrum for a nation which has still to sign a peace treaty with the United Kingdom, currently the only supplier of proven STOVL aircraft. Although the Spanish Naval Air Arm operates the US Marine Corps AV-8A version of the Harrier, this variant lacks naval radar and it is certain that the Argentinian Navy would want to use the aircraft for air defence rather than strike.

Light embarked helicopters also represent a problem for the Argentinians. An order for the Westland Lynx was cancelled as a result of the Falklands War and a replacement type has not been easy to find. Both the French SA.365F Dauphin II and the Italian-built Agusta-Bell AB.212 have been mentioned, but a decision has yet to be made. The single remaining Lynx, delivered before Argentina broke off normal relations with the UK, would probably be transferred

with the two Type 42 guided missile destroyers should they ever find a home.

Brazil is the other South American member of the carrier club, also operating a former British ship which has now been tasked solely with anti-submarine warfare duties. *Minas Gerais*, launched a year later than *25 de Mayo*, in 1944, is also due for replacement. Although a light aircraft carrier has been considered, financial constraints probably mean that Brazil's only way of keeping aircraft afloat in any numbers is to buy an American Arapaho merchant ship conversion capable of operating helicopters and perhaps STOVL aircraft. The useful life of *Minas Gerais* is expected to expire in about 1993, by which time a number of far-reaching decisions about the future of naval aviation will have to have been made. For example, control of the fixed-wing anti-submarine Trackers (and their potential replacements) might move to the navy, following the decision in January 1986 to give the Brazilian Army its own aviation corps. Funding remains the greatest hurdle, however. Although money has been found for the upgrading of the existing SH-3D helicopters to ASH-3H standard by Agusta, the new V28-class frigates have yet to receive their helicopters; a further order for Westland Lynxes is expected once funds are available.

Brazil's continued commitment to seaborne air power is further evidence of the fact that the aircraft carrier concept is far from dead. While almost every warship over 1,500 tons in the world is now equipped to operate helicopters, the cost of new-build aircraft carriers – even of the light CVS type – is more than many nations can hope to afford. Some countries have found a cost-effective way of taking helicopters, particularly ASW types, to sea, using fleet auxiliaries and other non-combatant vessels. In recent years the South African Navy, almost devoid of sources of equipment for anything more than a coastal navy, has embarked Super Frelon and now Puma helicopters in the support ship *Tafelberg*. The Super Frelon, a French design which is currently undergoing a life extension programme for the Aéronavale and future shore-based service, also serves at sea with the People's Liberation Army of China, and it is thought that several reconditioned and surplus French examples have been transferred to the PRC, where they are being used to give embarked experience to aircrew.

The carrier club now comprises nine nations operating 29 ships, or 42 if France's *Jeanne d'Arc* and the 12 amphibious carriers of the US Navy are taken into account. Argentina, Brazil, Chile, France, India, the Soviet Union and the United States plan to acquire additional or replacement carriers, whether transferred from other navies or new-build vessels. This, and the fact that another 29 nations also embark helicopters on smaller ships, leaves no doubt that naval aviation is vital to seagoing powers.

Seen during a flight deck firefighting exercise, Brazil's only aircraft carrier, *Minas Gerais*, is pictured with an untypical HB 350B Esquilo on deck. The carrier normally embarks S-2 Trackers and SH-3 Sea Kings (*Brazilian Navy*)

Apart from its fleet carriers, the US Navy has a powerful force of aviation-capable amphibious assault ships. This is USS *Iwo Jima*, lead ship of a class that is due to be replaced by the new *Wasp* and her ten sisters in the 1990s. (*US Navy*)

Soviet submarine propulsion: signs of a great leap forward?

Cdr Roy Corlett RN

Roy Corlett joined the Royal Navy as an artificer in 1937 and subsequently served in submarines in all rates and ranks up to commander. His final RN appointment was as Staff Weapons Officer to Flag Officer Submarines. Following retirement he worked for Vickers Shipbuilding Ltd before setting up as a consultant to companies such as the torpedo manufacturers Gould of the USA and Whitehead of Italy.

Soviet Victor II-class attack submarine, incorporating compliant tiling, contra-rotating propellers and stern-mounted pod.

The first Victor-class fleet submarine was laid down in 1965 and entered service in 1967–68. A total of 16 were built at a rate of two a year, with the class completed in 1974. Victor II was an enlarged version of Victor I; seven were built, the first appearing in 1972. Victor III was even larger. To date 20 have been built in rapid succession; the first was completed in 1978 and the last in 1984. The Victors were the first Soviet submarines to be designed specifically to attack both surface and submerged targets. They were also the first nuclear fleet boats to incorporate many new technologies: an Albacore hull and carefully profiled fin, both meticulously shaped to reduce underwater drag; provision for closing off all fin and casing free-flood holes when dived in order to maintain a sleek underwater shape; and compliant tiling overall, to reduce drag further and maintain a laminar flow of water past the hull. As time passed and pictures were taken of vessels at sea, new mysteries emerged. Why combine contra-rotating propellers on centreline shafting with two auxiliary propulsors? Why are the four-bladed contra-rotating propellers utterly different in design from the radically skewed multi-bladed propulsors considered indispensable to silent propulsion in the West? But above all, what is inside that very large streamlined pod mounted on the rudder structure of the Victor IIIs?

This article advances an uncomfortable thesis: that the Victor class was a testbed for the development of the drag-reduction techniques and new methods of propulsion now being applied to subsequent Soviet submarine types such as the Sierra and Akula. With a speed of over 42kt and a maximum diving depth in the order of half a mile, the Alfa class can already outperform British and American nuclear submarines. With the application of the new underwater technologies developed in the Soviet Union over the last 20 years, her latest attack submarines may be able to travel deeper and even faster.

Drag and turbulence

The energy needed to propel a submarine is dissipated in overcoming three main types of impedance:
● The resistance of the molecules of water to being thrust aside by the submarine's passage through the sea.
● Friction between the surface area of the submarine and the water flow.
● The drag effect behind the stern, rudders and propellers, created as the separated molecules of water rejoin each other.

Between submarine and sea there is a boundary layer, within which the movement of water molecules past the hull takes place. If the molecular movement is in well ordered sheets, then the flow is laminar and energy loss arises only from the friction between molecules and hull: the rougher the surfaces, the greater the drag. Any surface discontinuity or protrusion into the laminar flow of the boundary layer – such as the fin, which encloses the masts and periscopes, or the hydroplanes, which control operating depth – will disturb the smooth passage of water past the hull and break it up into a series of random motions which can more than double the drag. This phenomenon is called "turbulence".

In addition to designing a submarine with a smooth exterior and carefully contouring all protuberances to delay the onset of turbulence, attention must be given to overall shape and the ratio of length to beam. The optimum shape, as determined by detailed evaluations with USS *Albacore* in the early 1950s, is the "teardrop", with an aspect (ie, length/beam) ratio of 8.5:1. *Skipjack* was the first American nuclear submarine to incorporate the lessons learned with

---

The stern pod fitted to the Sierra class appears to be identical with but about 40% bigger than that of the Victors.

and a single electric propulsion motor to produce a massive 47,000shp: these advanced developments provided many areas for technical failure. But by the late 1970s the Soviets appeared to have solved their development and manufacturing difficulties, and by 1983 six Alfas were at sea. It is now a well documented fact that their maximum dived speed exceeds 42kt and operating depth 3,000ft.

If the Alfa is compared with the *Skipjack* class, some interesting conclusions can be reached:

	Alfa	Skipjack
Dived displacement	3,700 tons	3,513 tons
Dimensions	79 × 10 × 7.6m	76 × 9.6 × 8.9m
Aspect ratio	8.9:1	9.2:1
Propulsion power	47,000shp	15,000shp
Maximum dived speed	42kt +	30kt +

With its beautifully contoured fin faired into the hull, and lacking fixed, fin-mounted hydroplanes – a source of drag and turbulence to be found in all American submarine designs – Alfa is the better shape. But assuming that both classes have comparable underwater drag and are of similar size, it is possible to calculate dived performance as a function of propulsion power. Since a three-dimensional volume is being thrust through the sea, the power required for a given

USS *Seawolf*, essentially a conventional boat with a nuclear heart. (*US Navy*)

USS *Skipjack*'s teardrop hull gave her a 10kt dived speed advantage over *Seawolf*. (*US Navy*)

Albacore. The results were startling. Compared with such conventional nuclear predecessors as the *Seawolf*, with twin shafts and long pressure hull, on the same power output of 15,000shp the single-screw, teardrop-shaped *Skipjack* had a maximum dived speed more than 10kt better. This advance took place between the mid-1950s, when *Seawolf* was at sea, and the early 1960s when the *Skipjack* class entered service. The Russians seem to have taken about the same length of time to note American technology, evaluate it in the Victor class, and incorporate the practical sea experience thus gained into the Alfa class.

The first Alfa was laid down in the mid-1960s and scrapped in 1974. The most likely reason for this short life was the incorporation of too much new technology into one vessel. A new titanium alloy for the hull and a structure able to withstand diving depths of at least 800m, and two liquid metal-cooled nuclear reactors of a new type combined with two steam turbo-alternators

The Albacore hull and sleek fairing of the Soviet Alfa class (above) contrast sharply with the extreme length/beam ratio, non-retractable forward planes and starkly vertical fin of USS *Los Angeles* (right). (*US Navy*)

speed is a cube function. Thus the power needed to double the speed of *Skipjack* from 30 to 60kt is calculated as follows:

Speed-increase ratio $= \dfrac{60}{30} = 2:1$

Cube of speed-increase ratio $= 2^3 = 8$

Power needed for 60kt $= 15,000$ (at 30kt) $\times 8 = 120,000$shp

Using this method, the power required to increase the speed of *Skipjack* (30kt) to that of Alfa (43kt) would be:

Speed-increase ratio $= \dfrac{43}{30} = 1.43:1$

Cube of speed-increase ratio $= 1.43^3 = 2.92:1$
Power needed $= 15,000 \times 2.92 = 43,863$shp

This is significantly less than the 47,000shp of the Alfa. So taking account of other design improvements in the latter, such as retractable forward hydroplanes (which are not needed at speeds above 10kt), careful fairing of all leading edges, and compliant tiling over the whole of the hull to reduce drag, it is possible that the Alfa's maximum dived speed approaches 44kt.

So far so good, but one major design problem arises: how to control waste heat. In power terms, 47,000shp is equal to 35MW, nearly ten times more than the output of the electric propulsion motors fitted in the largest diesel-electric submarine. Ignoring the prime mover, the electrical efficiency of the two alternators and the propulsion motor is probably about 90%. Thus 10% of 35MW, 3.5MW, is an energy loss which is dissipated as heat. To use a homely analogy, this is equivalent to trying to cool 3,500 1kW electric bar fires in a fairly confined space, something very difficult to achieve. However, if the latest classes of Soviet submarine are fitted with superconductivity machinery, electric heating power losses disappear.

Superconductivity

If an electrical conductor is cooled to within a few degrees of absolute zero, $-273°C$, all electrical resistance disappears. Since it is ohmic resistance which generates heat when current passes, a state of superconductivity means that significantly greater power can be developed within a much smaller weight and volume of electric motor. Although the principle of superconductivity has been known since 1911, the technology for its application has been developed only in the last 20 years.

The availability of liquid helium as a medium for heat extraction down to very low temperatures, compact cryogenic refrigeration plants and efficient thermal shielding were the keys which converted experimental laboratory equipment into production hardware. In early 1974 US Naval Sea Systems Command (NAVSEA) ordered a ship's electrical propulsion plant incorporating superconducting motors and generators. By June 1977 the US Naval Ship Research and Development Centre had successfully completed tests of the first of two 3,000shp superconducting motors. By 1979 there were reports that NAVSEA was aiming for superconductive propulsion systems of up to 60MW per shaft. Nothing is known about the outcome of this project. But what is obvious from the mass of unclassified Soviet technical literature – translated and readily available to Western countries – is that in the 1960s and 1970s the USSR was rapidly overtaking America in all areas of underwater research, including cryogenics and superconductivity.

According to "Superconducting Electrical Machinery", a paper published by Engineer V. Viktorov in 1976, for a shaft output of 25.9MW a superconducting electric motor is 53 tons lighter and 9–14% less bulky than a conventional steam turbine drive via reduction gearbox. Fully 95% of the power passes to the propellers, with only 5% needed for helium compressors, liquefiers and ancillary machinery. On the assumption that of this 5% not more than one tenth turns into "wild" heat, the heat management system is only called on to reject $25.9 \times 005 = 147.5$kW. So, although there is no positive proof that superconducting electrical machinery is fitted in the Alfa class, there is plenty of evidence to suggest that it may be. Conversely, if the propulsion system is conventional, it would be interesting to know how a giant-sized 35MW electric propulsion motor can be contained within a pressure hull as compact as the Alfa's, and how 3.5MW of heating losses are extracted and dissipated.

Propulsion

In most modern submarines the shaft output is translated to motion through the sea via a single propeller. In all American and most British submarines this has at least seven deeply skewed blades and rotates comparatively slowly, an arrangement said to reduce cavitation and thus the acoustic noise which passive sonar can detect. But the price is a reduction in coupling efficiency. Another problem is torque reaction. This appears in two forms, both of which increase drag:

● The power output of the propeller produces a twist reaction on the submarine's hull which must be counteracted with rudder and hydroplane bias. This wastes propulsive power.
● Screwing water through the propeller blades, and imparting large quantities of energy to the water molecules in the process, generates wake turbulence in the form of vortices, increasing propeller drag and reducing thrust.

The Victor III-class submarines are each fitted with a pair of four-bladed tandem propellers on a common shaft, and it is possible that the Alfa and later classes have the same arrangement.

Jet propulsion

Over the last 25 years Soviet technical literature on underwater propulsion has contained frequent references to a number of advanced concepts:
● Magnetohydrodynamic propulsion (MHD), ramjet engines and MHD induction compressors.
● Superconductivity and its application to electromagnetic propulsion.
● "Skin motors" which propel by means of surface rippling of a flexible skin, as in the skate family of fish.

Two of the most definitive papers on ramjets and skin motors are an article by Capt-Lt A. Popov entitled "Submarine and Sea Skates" and published in Moscow in August 1974, and "Magnetohydrodynamic Engines," published in *Morskoy Sbornik*, the Soviet naval journal, in 1970. They came at the right time to have been applicable to the many testbed modifications made to the Victor I, II and III classes during their evaluation and could explain the very large stern-mounted pod first seen on the Victor IIIs and now a feature of the new Sierra and Akula classes.

The MHD propulsion pod

The illustration shows a two-stage enlargement of the Victor III tail pod. The lower cross-section shows how the system probably works; the dimensions were derived from range data and scaling from other known parameters. The second picture is an enlargement of a section of the pod inner wall and surrounds, showing component parts. These are as follows:
● Through the centre of the pod runs a tube with a venturi entrance. When the submarine is on the surface the tube entrance is protected by a streamlined cover (shown dotted in the diagram).
● On the inner surface of the tube is an annular composite structure consisting of inductor coils and a resilient flexible sheath partitioned into segments, each of which is filled with a Ferro (ie, magnetic) fluid. The sheath and inductor coils are separated by cavities partitioned to match the resilient sheath segments.
● Surrounding the propulsion tube are liquid helium cooling coils to reduce the inductor winding temperatures to the point of superconductivity, a vacuum gap to prevent thermal leakage, and further layers of thermal insulation.

In operation, a static inverter would convert direct current into a voltage variation, which would pass through the inductor coil and generate a pulsed magnetic field. This would in turn act on the ferro fluid, setting up a travelling wave in the fluid and

MHD Propulsion pod

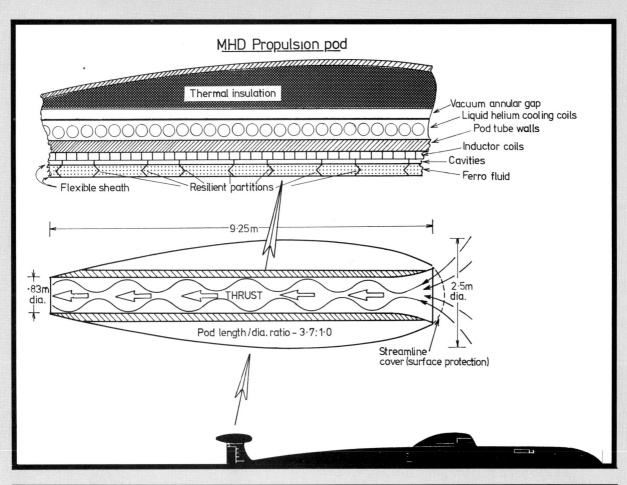

Thermal insulation

Vacuum annular gap
Liquid helium cooling coils
Pod tube walls
Inductor coils
Cavities
Ferro fluid

Flexible sheath — Resilient partitions

9·25 m

·83 m dia.

THRUST

2·5 m dia.

Pod length/dia. ratio – 3·7:1·0

Streamline cover (surface protection)

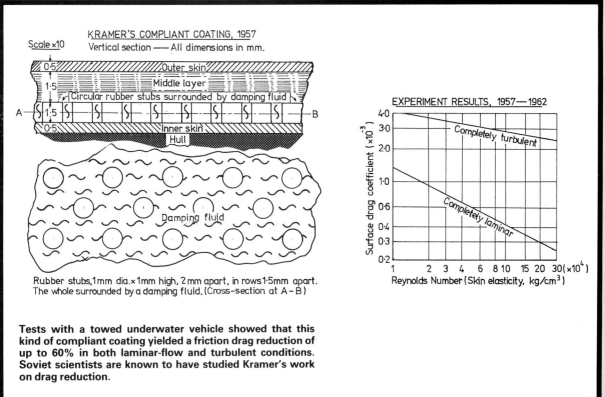

Scale ×10

KRAMER'S COMPLIANT COATING, 1957

Vertical section —— All dimensions in mm.

0·5 — Outer skin
1·5 — Middle layer
Circular rubber stubs surrounded by damping fluid
A — 1·5 — B
0·5 — Inner skin
Hull

Damping fluid

Rubber stubs, 1mm dia. × 1mm high, 2mm apart, in rows 1·5mm apart. The whole surrounded by a damping fluid. (Cross-section at A – B)

EXPERIMENT RESULTS, 1957—1962

Surface drag coefficient (×10⁻³)

Completely turbulent

Completely laminar

Reynolds Number (Skin elasticity, kg/cm³)

Tests with a towed underwater vehicle showed that this kind of compliant coating yielded a friction drag reduction of up to 60% in both laminar-flow and turbulent conditions. Soviet scientists are known to have studied Kramer's work on drag reduction.

thence in the flexible sheath. The resulting motion would draw in water at the tube venturi entrance and expel it at the rear to create thrust. It is calculated that enough propulsive power could be generated to give a dived cruising speed of up to 7kt.

This description is pure supposition, but there is evidence to support it. The tube lining and inductor coil structure are as described and illustrated in Soviet Patent No 457629, describing a wave-engine device and first published in 1975 by K. I. Kim, A. A. Afonin and V. I. Bondarenko of the Soviet Institute of Electrodynamics. This may have been based on the results of Kramer's experiments, carried out between 1957 and 1962; the operating principle is certainly very similar. Apart from being used for propulsion, as

outlined above, the ripple effect could also be exploited by fitting such a system in the form of a compliant outer skin to a submarine's hull. Drag could then be reduced significantly by relating ripple frequency to dived speed. More exciting still, the two functions could be combined to produce both drag reduction and propulsion. Is this what Popov was referring to in his article "Submarines and Sea Skates"?

USS *Billfish* of the *Sturgeon* class (below) **and the Royal Navy ballistic missile submarine HMS *Renown*** (bottom) **typify Western nuclear submarine design philosophies. Did their appearance stimulate the Soviets into their present spectacular advances?** (*Royal Navy*)

The state of the Soviet submarine art

In assessing contemporary Soviet submarine developments, much can be learned from the available mass of photographs and unclassified data. From Victor I onwards, hulls have been carefully contoured to generate minimum drag. Fins are curved to fair into the hull structure; all apertures in free-flood areas are sealed and streamlined when dived. All external surfaces are tiled with compliant coating, further to reduce surface friction. Although tandem propellers have been observed only on the Victors, it would be logical to fit the same arrangement on later classes; in addition to the advantages already claimed, they are more efficient and can transmit greater power than a single screw before the onset of cavitation. The forward propeller can be visualised as a supercharger imparting its energy to the after unit, which carries out further compression and unwinds the vortices. What has been described as a MHD propulsion pod on the Victor IIIs is now fitted to Sierra and Akula-class boats – a sure sign that, whatever it is, it works. And the way an icing coat forms on the superstructures of some submarines within minutes of surfacing seems to indicate cryogenics in some form or another.

There are many indications of Soviet advances in underwater technology. But why should this be so? According to Western reports, Russian submarines are large, cumbersome and easy to detect because they are noisy. One possible explanation might lie in the fact that during 1957–67, when the Soviets were struggling to solve the problems of their first generation of nuclear submarines, America commissioned eight classes of nuclear submarines totalling 39 vessels, followed by 37 of the *Sturgeon* class. From keel-laying to commissioning, the average build time was less than three years. The US was also declaring its interest in drag-reduction applications such as compliant coatings, long-chain polymers and surfactants, and in new propulsion concepts like magnetohydrodynamic pulse propulsion and water jets. The development of high-yield steels was openly discussed, and titanium alloys seemed imminent. With an optimism typical of the period, it was declared that by the 1980s submarine speeds of 50–60kt would be commonplace. Such a massive advance on all underwater technological fronts must have appeared a great threat to the Soviets, who seem to have made extraordinary endeavours to catch up.

There now seems a strong possibility that the USSR has not only succeeded in drawing level but is now in advance of America and Britain. Why this should have happened is beyond the scope of this article, although it is legitimate to express concern over current Western attitudes. The Russians are not ten feet tall, nor are they supermen. But is it not equally ridiculous to claim that the West always has the best and that it will remain so?

France's commitment to a nuclear navy

First published in *Jane's Defence Weekly*.

Ingénieur en Chef de l'Armement Tournyol du Clos

Rubis, the French Navy's first nuclear fleet submarine. (**Marius Bar**)

More than 30 years after USS *Nautilus* went through her first trials, nuclear propulsion still shares with supersonic flight the rare distinction of being both a remarkable military success and a total commercial failure. The civilian nuclear fleet is currently limited to three Soviet quasi-naval icebreakers, compared with more than 350 military vessels (mostly submarines). And the rate of construction does not appear to be slowing in any of the five nuclear navies.

France's nuclear fleet, although only the fourth largest, is unusual in respect of its structure and of the design of the reactors used.

The go-ahead for studies in nuclear propulsion in France was given in 1955. The year had begun with the transmission of a historic message from *Nautilus* at 11.00 on January 17: "Under way on nuclear power". In February the French Government decided to authorise the construction of a nuclear submarine, the hull of which was christened Q-244, at the Cherbourg Naval Dockyard.

Nuclear fleets (as at January 1, 1984)

	SSBN			SSN			Aircraft carriers			Cruisers			Others
	O	C	P	O	C	P	O	C	P	O	C	P	
USSR	64	5	—	118	3	—	—	1	—	1	1	—	2
USA	34	2	5	89	9	10	4	3	1	9	—	—	4
UK	4	—	4	13	1	4	—	—	—	—	—	—	—
France	5	1	1	2	3	3	—	—	1	—	—	—	—
China	—	1	—	2	2	—	—	—	—	—	—	—	—

O: operational, C: under construction, P: projected

A nuclear reactor works by establishing and controlling a chain reaction. Each time the nucleus of a uranium atom is split, energy is released in the form of heat, and neutrons are given off to split other nuclei in turn. But not all the neutrons produced in this way can be used to maintain the chain reaction. In particular, a certain number of them try to escape from the reactor. Neutrons with extra energy (known as "fast neutrons") escape more easily than those of low energy ("slow neutrons").

The reactor designer therefore has two choices:
● Direct use of fast neutrons, making up for the increased leakage through extra production. The resulting system is known as a fast-breeder reactor, the neutron leakage being used to produce fuel outside the core. Such reactors are often termed "super-generators".
● A slow neutron reactor, in which the fission neutrons are slowed down to improve the economy of the reaction by plunging the core into a moderator.

The fluid which serves to extract the energy from the core is known as the calo-carrier. In 1955 the Americans chose a pressurised water reactor for *Nautilus*. In this system water was both the moderator and the calo-carrier. Built in parallel was a second submarine, *Seawolf*, powered by a beryllium-moderated reactor with liquid sodium cooling agent.

The French had some experience, going back to the pre-war period, with heavy water, which is in some respects a better moderator than natural or light water. In fact natural water absorbs some of the neutrons emitted at the time of fission and thus dictates the use of light enriched fuels; heavy water, being less absorbent, makes it possible to use natural uranium directly as a fuel.

Since the technique of uranium enrichment was unavailable in France at that time, the logical choice was a natural uranium reactor moderated by heavy water. Theoretical studies for the reactor, preparations for the construction of its components, and the production of the submarine hull at Cherbourg were all launched in parallel. Unfortunately, after two years the work came to a stop. The use of natural uranium had led to a core too big for a submarine. Much had been learned, however, while most of the hull sections were subsequently used in the building of the experimental submarine *Gymnote*.

Parallel technology-transfer negotiations with the Americans also came to nothing, though in May 1959 France and the USA did reach an agreement whereby the latter provided enriched uranium for use in a prototype land-based nuclear submarine boiler.

The teams which had worked on the Q-244 project were redeployed within the nuclear propulsion department of the Commissariat à l'Energie Atomique (CEA), and on August 15, 1964, a land-based prototype (PAT) was started up at Cadarache. The

Gymnote, **test boat for France's submarine-launched missile systems.**

theoretical and production work on this reactor had taken less than five years. The prototype land-based nuclear boiler for the first British nuclear submarine, built under US licence, had begun operating in 1963. Meanwhile, the establishment of a plant capable of uranium enrichment by gaseous diffusion at Pierrelatte ensured that there would be enough nuclear fuel for the submarines now on the slips at Cherbourg.

The land-based prototype at Cadarache is mounted in a submarine hull section immersed in a pool to make it as representative as possible of the production version. The reactor is of the pressurised water variety, with natural water acting as moderator and calo-carrier. The water extracts the energy generated in the vessel by circulating across the core, where it is heated up, and then goes on to the steam generator. There it transfers its heat to the water in a closed circuit comprising steam turbines and a condenser. This secondary water is vapourised into steam to drive the

turbines before being condensed back into liquid form. Thus the engine, which sees only uncontaminated secondary water, can be situated outside the confines of the reactor. To prevent leakage, the primary water is maintained under pressure, whence the designation "pressurised water reactor".

PAT is a loop reactor: ie, the two steam generators are separate from the reactor vessel and are linked to it by loops of piping incorporating the pumps which circulate the primary water.

The prototype at Cadarache was followed by a series of production systems fitted to the nuclear ballistic

missile submarines which now form the spearhead of the National Deterrent Force. The accompanying table shows when work began on these boats and when they entered service. The new SSBN *L'Inflexible* is included, although it officially belongs to a different class, because its nuclear propulsion system is in fact the latest version of PAT. Assuming an active working life of around 25 years for *L'Inflexible*, a span of half a century will separate the first studies of the prototype from the withdrawal from service of the last reactor of the series.

Though the external appearance of the nuclear boiler will have changed little over these 50 years, the performance of the nuclear fuel has increased

French SSBNs

Name	Date laid down	Date commissioned
Le Redoutable	November 1964	December 1, 1971
Le Terrible	June 22, 1967	December 1, 1973
Le Foudroyant	December 1969	June 6, 1974
L'Indomptable	December 4, 1971	December 31, 1976
Le Tonnant	October 1974	April 3, 1980
L'Inflexible	March 27, 1980	January 1985

significantly. The first core to power *Le Redoutable* remained usable for almost six years; the latest cores are designed to last for 25 years, practically the whole working life of a submarine.

Although the PAT has been seen as a success since the early 1970s, the CEA and Directorate of Naval Shipbuilding engineers have long since begun to think about the next generation of shipboard nuclear boiler. This is likely to exploit the phenomenon of convection. When a vessel full of water is heated from beneath, circulation is created by convection; the lighter hot water rises, cools at the surface and descends again. Placing the steam generator above the reactor vessel should result in natural circulation of the primary water: heated in the core, this rises by convection to the steam-generator, where it cools on transferring its heat to the secondary water. The cooler primary water then descends once again to the core. This system does away with primary pumps, to a certain degree at least, and has three principal advantages:
• Reactor reliability is improved by eliminating dependence on the primary pumps.
• The submarine is quieter; as with all moving parts, the primary pumps are a source of radiated noise.
• The reactor takes up less space.

However, the steam generator and internal structure of the core are much more complex to produce. A new

prototype therefore appeared necessary. This was the advanced prototype boiler (CAP), which began operating for the first time at the end of 1975, alongside PAT.

In contrast with the first prototype, no attempt was made to simulate CAP's eventual working environment, for two reasons. First, it was considered that the problems of installing nuclear powerplants in submarines had been satisfactorily solved with PAT and its production offspring. Second, the French national electricity supply organisation (Electricité de France) had opted for pressurised-water reactors and wanted to use CAP for trials.

CAP gave rise to a family of projects for production advanced boilers (CAS). Identical in principle to CAP, they would vary in capacity according to the size of the vessels they were to power. In the end the first development to go ahead was a small powerplant for a nuclear attack submarine based on the *Agosta*-class patrol submarine.

These submarines (SNA), with a displacement of about 2,700 tonnes compared with the 3,700 tonnes of the Soviet Alfa class, the 5,000 tonnes of the British *Trafalgar* class and 7,000 tonnes of the American *Los Angeles* class, constitute a definite technical achievement. With the exception of a deep-diving nuclear research submarine, the *No 1*, and the *Tullibee*,

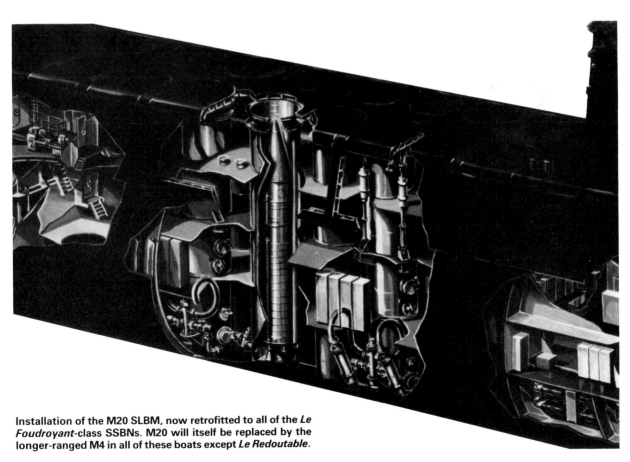

Installation of the M20 SLBM, now retrofitted to all of the *Le Foudroyant*-class SSBNs. M20 will itself be replaced by the longer-ranged M4 in all of these boats except *Le Redoutable*.

French nuclear attack submarines

Name	Date laid down	Date commissioned
Rubis	December 11, 1976	February 23, 1983
Saphir	September 1, 1979	July 1984
SNA3	September 1981	March 1987
SNA4	October 1982	November 1988
SNA5	early 1984	October 1990

another experimental model (both American), they are the smallest nuclear submarines ever produced. A total of eight (originally five) of these *Rubis*-class boats are to be built.

France is currently engaged in two new programmes for nuclear-propelled vessels: a new-generation submarine and an aircraft carrier. They have one feature in common: their nuclear propulsion systems. The costs of developing a new reactor have risen, so that efforts are being made to apply one system to a variety of vehicles. This approach is not new: the first US nuclear aircraft carrier was fitted with no fewer than eight reactors directly derived from the nuclear submarine system.

In the case of *Richelieu*, the new French aircraft carrier, two reactors will be enough for propulsion, the on-board auxiliary systems and, if necessary, the catapults. A single reactor will equip the nuclear submarines.

The carriers apart, the great majority of future French nuclear-powered naval vessels will be submarines, whatever weapon systems they carry. Nuclear propulsion offers this type of vessel a range of operational capabilities so much more comprehensive than does traditional propulsion that it is difficult to imagine how the submarine of the future could not be nuclear. As far as surface ships are concerned, the development of nuclear propulsion is affected by a number of factors:

• The tonnage of the vessels: given the current state of the technology, it appears difficult to "nuclearise" vessels of less than 5,000 tonnes, a category of ship relatively rare in the French Navy (frigates of the *Tourville* type and above).

• The cost of petroleum products and the availability of substitutes.

• The lessons that the navy will draw from the operational use of its first nuclear aircraft carrier.

If this experience proves positive, one could imagine at the beginning of the 21st century a French surface fleet comprising two aircraft carriers, three or four escort frigates for the carriers, and a fleet of support vessels, all nuclear-powered. In fact the French Navy's support tankers, and the maintenance and repair ships of the *Jules Verne* type, are relatively large vessels which have to be deployed great distances, quickly and for long periods without consuming the very stores that they must distribute to operational ships. They could thus prove very susceptible to nuclearisation.

The last 30 years have seen the emergence of the pressurised water reactor as the French Navy's primary propulsion system. However, according to *Jane's Fighting Ships*, the remarkable speed performance of the most recent Soviet nuclear attack submarine, the Alfa class, is due to the adoption of a new type of liquid metal-cooled reactor. The characteristics of liquid metals permit the achievement of an increased power-weight ratio for the propulsion system, though at the cost of certain other disadvantages which led the Americans to abandon their own comparable programme, tested in *Seawolf* in 1956–1958.

It is now possible that this success, if confirmed, will lead US and Western navies to turn to this type of reactor for their future generations of submarines. We may therefore be on the threshold of a minor technological revolution in the field of shipboard reactors.

Left: **Launch of *Saphir*, second of the *Rubis*-class fleet submarines. She was commissioned in 1984.** (*ECP Armees*)

Below: **Tank model of the first French nuclear-powered aircraft carrier, to be known as *Richelieu*.** (*DTCN*)

Soviet Navy: the king is dead . . .

First published in *Jane's Defence Weekly*.

Yossef Bodansky

A routine announcement of an official visit to Tunisia late last year revealed that Admiral of the Fleet Vladimir Nikolayevich Chernavin had become the Commander-in-Chief of the Soviet Navy, in succession to the towering figure of Admiral Sergei Gorshkov, and a Deputy Minister of Defence. Chernavin has been considered as the heir apparent ever since his unprecedented promotion to Admiral of the Fleet in November 1983. At that time he was also awarded the Hero of the Soviet Union title for his contribution to the development of the Soviet Fleet.

Admiral V. N. Chernavin is one of the leading members of the new generation of young senior officers which arose from the revival of Soviet military families. He was born in 1928 to an officer in the Northern Fleet, and joined the fleet soon after the war. He insisted on serving in the Northern Fleet in order to preserve the family tradition. His career centred on submarines and he advanced from lieutenant and navigator aboard a submarine to Commander-in-Chief of the Northern Fleet.

In 1962 Chernavin led the first major cruise of Soviet nuclear submarines in the Arctic, developing new methods for communication, navigation, and surfacing from under the ice. Meanwhile, he maintained a relatively high profile in the Soviet military press, featuring regularly from 1957 onwards as a good commander, a good organiser, and, most importantly, as an outstanding Party worker.

His overall record and political standing helped him overcome the effects of late-1962 "mistakes" in training which were serious enough to be criticised on the pages of *Morskoi Sbornik*, the fleet publication. A few months later he was described as a "good officer" in *Krasnaya Zvezda*.

He graduated from the Naval Academy in 1965, and from the Voroshilov Academy of the General Staff in 1969. In late 1975 he was nominated the Chief of Staff of the Northern Fleet, and on July 1, 1977, he became the Commander of the Northern Fleet. He held this post until December 16, 1981.

While in the Northern Fleet, Chernavin contributed regularly to the Soviet military press. As a submariner he emphasised the significance of the oceangoing

Admiral of the Fleet Vladimir Nikolayevich Chernavin, the new Commander-in-Chief of the Soviet Navy. He shares the views of his predecessor, Admiral Gorshkov, on the strategic significance of the Red Fleet but insists that it must be fully integrated into a combined-arms command structure.

submarines of the Northern Fleet. However, Party-political themes dominated most of his writings, in which he demonstrated loyalty and political orthodoxy. Many of his "patriotic" speeches were quoted as examples of the correct balance between professional and political themes.

The significance of the positions advocated by Chernavin as a senior commander of the fleet, and which will determine his tenure as C-in-C of the Soviet Fleet, becomes apparent when his previous career as a submariner intimately involved in the use and

Gorshkov's legacy to Chernavin includes a capable and expanding escort force. Latest destroyer classes are the complementary *Sovremennys*, optimised for surface warfare, and the ASW *Udaloys*. Principal weapon system of the *Sovremenny*-class *Osmotritelny* (above) is the SS-N-22 anti-ship missile. *Vitse-Admiral Kulakov* of the *Udaloy* class (below) is armed for anti-submarine warfare with two quad launchers for the SS-N-44 missile system, a pair of Helix helicopters, two RBU 6000 12-barrelled rocket launchers, and eight 21in torpedo tubes.

command of nuclear missile-carrying submarines (SSBNs) is considered. Throughout this time Chernavin operated submarines of the Northern Fleet with almost complete operational and tactical autonomy, being responsible for matching the operational profiles of the submarines to their performance.

At the same time, however, these SSBNs constituted an integral part of the Soviet nuclear arsenal. The employment of these submarines and their ballistic missiles was part of a unified war plan under the direct command and control of the land-based Strategic Rocket Forces. This taught Chernavin that it is possible for naval forces to operate effectively as an integral part of a national land-based command without losing the operational and tactical autonomy needed to exploit fully the unique performance of naval weapon systems.

Soon after his nomination in December 1981 as the first Deputy C-in-C of the Fleet and the Chief of the Main Naval Staff, Chernavin launched a debate on the future art of war for the Soviet fleet in *Morskoi Sbornik*. The main argument concerned the degree of integration of the fleet into combined-arms operations. Chernavin was determined to ensure that the fleet would not be left behind in the intensifying revolution in military affairs initiated by Marshal Ogarkov.

In September 1981, still under Chernavin's command, the Northern Fleet played a central role in the ZAPAD-81 exercise, performing the largest naval landing in Soviet history. The Soviets consider ZAPAD-81 to typify a future war, and Chernavin saw that only a complete integration of the fleet into the emerging strategy of the USSR would assure its development. His experience as a submariner convinced him that such an integration into a combined-arms high command would not cost the operational autonomy of the fleet.

In his January 1982 article in *Morskoi Sbornik* Chernavin reiterated the need for a thorough re-examination of "questions of the theory of the navy" but disagreed with the prevailing view, usually identified as Gorshkov's, that the navy should have an independent art of war. He emphasised that the lack of unified views on theoretical problems throughout the whole of the Soviet armed forces could result in serious difficulties in practice.

Chernavin further emphasised that "there are no purely independent spheres of armed struggle". Each combat arm is able to exercise influence on the enemy in its own physical environment – on land, in the air, on the water and under the water. He insisted that victory "is attained by the joint effort of all combat arms which evokes the necessity to integrate all knowledge on armed struggle within the framework of a unified military science."

Soon afterwards, senior officers of the Soviet Navy went even further in their call for its integration into a unified combined-arms art of war. Capt 1st Rank V. Shlomin claimed in April 1983 that "under modern conditions, the unity of the armed struggle is expressed in a greater degree thanks to the objective requirements and the possibility of mutual penetration of combat arms to the sphere of activities of the other combat arms.

"The navy has substantially increased operational-tactical options for activities in the sea and in the air, and equipped with nuclear missile weapons has acquired the capability to operate throughout the entire territory of the enemy, taking part in the solution of strategic missions. . . .

"The direction of building and strategic employment of the Navy, as for each and every other combat arm of the armed forces, is set primarily by the policy, military doctrine of the state, and the emergence from them of a unified military strategy."

In July 1984, in an analysis in *Voyenno Istoricheskiy Zhurnal* of the activities of the Main Naval Staff (GMSh) during the Great Patriotic War, Chernavin introduced a clear distinction between the respective roles of the GMSh and the ground forces-oriented Supreme High Command (VGK). He attributes the success of the combat operations of the fleet to "the high level of operational-tactical views established in

the fleet . . . and (the) flexibility and mobility of the control-management organs, including the GMSh."

The main achievements of the GMSh lay in the training of the naval personnel, the acquisition of weapon systems and their introduction into operational use, and the development of tactics for their combat use.

At the strategic-operational level, the officers of the GMSh made a significant contribution to success through their efforts "to strengthen contact with the fleets and clearly co-ordinate actions with the maritime groupings of ground forces. This was greatly aided by close contact with the Soviet Army General Staff."

Thus, even senior naval officers recognise that the Soviet Navy has become a subsystem within the organisational framework of the combined-arms armed forces. It could therefore function only as an integral part of a larger formation, carrying out specific combat operations independently, like any

other specialised combat arm, should the need arise.

Chernavin emphasises that the distinction between a dominating combined-arms VGK and general staff, and a specialised GMSh, is still valid even though the present-day fleet has "operational-strategic capabilities and is capable of carrying out strategic tasks in fighting against a strong sea enemy." This perception of the role of the fleet fits closely with the view of a centralised and unified high command advocated by Ogarkov. In his book *History Teaches Vigilance*, Ogarkov held that the recent increase in the range and power of highly mobile weapon systems made them potentially decisive: "At present, the combat capabilities of troops, aviation and the fleet, the long range of their weapons and their manoeuvrability have sharply increased. The periods required to concentrate strike groupings . . . have been reduced . . . The military supreme high command has obtained the capability of directly and decisively influencing the course and the outcome of the war." Ogarkov concluded that as a result of "the development of military-technical resources" any war in the near future "will acquire unprecedented spatial scope, encompass entire continents and ocean expanses."

Admiral Gorshkov gave a comprehensive interview in the July 1985 issue of *Voyenno Istoricheskiy Zhurnal*, which can be considered as a summing up of his

---

Two of the means by which the Soviet Navy could perform the tasks listed by Admiral Gorshkov in summing up his career: the cruiser *Slava*, armed with a huge battery of long-range anti-carrier missiles (below), and the amphibious assault ship *Ivan Rogov* (below left). (*Royal Navy*)

lengthy active command of the navy. Under his command "the fleet has been transformed into a reliable shield of the country through the will of the party and the people. A component part of the armed forces, it is capable, both together with other services of the armed forces and independently, of fulfilling its strategic and operational tasks in the maritime theatres of military operations.

"The contemporary fleet is able to strike important ground targets of the enemy; destroy enemy forces at sea and in bases; support the ground forces with nuclear missile strikes and assault-landing forces from the sea; repel enemy assault-landing forces from the sea; disrupt the naval communications of the enemy, and protect its own communications.

"A great strike power, high manoeuvrability of groups of ships and aircraft, enormous range of operations, capability to quickly and secretly deploy forces and carry out crushing strikes against ground and sea targets, constant combat readiness of units and formations, and high professional and unwavering ideological staunchness of its personnel are the main characteristics of the fleet." It is significant that the above definition owes more to Chernavin than to the traditional principles advocated for decades by Gorshkov.

In an *Izvestiya* interview on July 27, 1985, Chernavin introduced a new definition of the sea might of the State, emphasising the integration of the fleet into unified combined-arms military operations. According to Chernavin, "sea might is the extent to which a particular state is able to make the most effective use of the oceans of the world, or the hydrosphere of the earth, as it is called. Sea might also includes the ability of the armed forces to protect this country against the threat of attack from seas or oceans."

Thus, with the nomination of Chernavin as the Fleet Commander-in-Chief, yet another advocate of the strategic concept identified with the works of Ogarkov has assumed a critical and senior position in the Soviet High Command.

US Navy:
full speed ahead . . .
but what course?

Vice-Adm M. S. Holcomb USN

USS *Carl Vinson*, third of the *Nimitz* class, under way in Californian waters. The nuclear-powered fleet carrier continues to be the capital ship of the US Navy.

"The more things change, the more they stay the same." At the midpoint of the 1980s, that old saw certainly applies to the US Navy. Because ships take a long time to build and longer to wear out, the fundamental character of the American fleet will change very little between now and the turn of the century. Two thirds of the ships that will comprise the fleet in the year 2000 are in service or under construction today. Collectively, those ships will define the kind of tasks the United States will be able to perform in warfare at sea or in dealing with crises short of global war.

During the past five years a lot has been said and written about the maritime aspects of US strategy, about achieving superiority at sea, and about the necessity for naval recovery. Building up the Navy has been a consistent goal of the Reagan Administration, in large part because, faced with parity in strategic nuclear weaponry and what is essentially a stalemate on the Central Front, the maritime is one of the few areas of superpower competition in which the United States can conceivably maintain (or regain, depending on one's viewpoint) a clear edge.

Once the dust of rhetoric settles, it becomes clear that US naval strategy has changed very little over three decades. It focuses on the emerging maritime threat posed by the Soviet Union and the need – with the help of allies – to deal with it more or less simultaneously in five principal ocean areas: the North-west Pacific, the Mediterranean, the Eastern and North Atlantic, the South China Sea, and the Indian Ocean. The first three have been the focus of intensive analysis, strategic planning and fleet exercising since the end of the Second World War. The latter two have assumed importance more recently as the Soviet Navy has begun operating in two strategically significant regions far from its home waters. Apart from the fact that shifting or "swinging" US naval forces from one ocean to another to meet the demands of a global strategy has been ruled out by the current administration, America's maritime strategy has been fairly constant. The issue has been one of priority in the application of available force.

"Naval superiority" may have been a useful concept when one country's ships of the line could be arrayed against those of another, but the notion becomes almost meaningless in the context of two dissimilar superpower maritime forces with completely different missions. The Soviet Navy – predominantly submarines and long-range anti-ship missile-equipped ships and aircraft – is, according to the best estimates, devoted to protecting certain sea areas for secure use by their ballistic missile submarines and to defending the homeland. It may be admirably suited to these tasks, but it is in no position to take on the American fleet in the open ocean. On the other hand, the US Navy – with carrier battle forces and amphibious capabilities as its centrepieces – is built primarily for the projection of power ashore, with the securing of selected sea areas to permit the safe passage of merchant traffic as a secondary role. Two questions therefore need to be answered. Which navy is more likely to carry out its missions successfully? And what will be the degree of interaction between them?

On the US side, the force structure has steadily declined to the point where the Navy's primary responsibilities could not all be met at the same time in a worldwide conflict with the Soviet Union. Although the much heralded drive to achieve a "600-ship Navy" by the end of the 1980s has not yet resulted in significant growth in the strength of the fleet's battle forces, a serious downward trend has been arrested. From the outset, the goal has been to increase from 12 to 15 the number of deployable carrier battle groups, to reactivate four battleships, to increase the

Above: **Building the 600-ship Navy: a near-complete USS *Ticonderoga* is shepherded past the *Kidd*-class destroyer USS *Callaghan*.**

Right: **Primary fighting unit of the US Navy is the carrier battle group. Here the nuclear-powered cruisers USS *Virginia* (foreground) and *California* escort the carriers *Eisenhower* and *Nimitz*. (*US Navy*)**

attack submarine force from 90 to 100, and to increase amphibious lift by a third. To do this in a balanced way would have required the construction of 25 new ships a year for a sustained period (in contrast to the average of 12 over the last dozen years, a building rate which has simply not proved feasible. An average of 17 new ships a year has emerged from the give and take which leads to annual budgets, of which only a third have gone to the deployable battle force. There have been significant qualitative improvements but, except for the return of two battleships, the conversion of a few early ballistic missile submarines to SSN configuration, and the delivery of 26 previously ordered frigates, little in the way of force expansion

has been achieved. At the end of fiscal year (FY) 1985 there were on order some 60 new ships which, as they deliver over the next four years, should fill out two additional carrier battle groups, add ten more frigates to the force and hold the nuclear attack submarine force at about 90 as large numbers of vessels built in the 1960s reach retirement age. Thus, though the capability of the fleet is increasing steadily, the force won't actually grow much larger.

Aircraft procurement has been similarly constrained. During the five Reagan budget years an average of 283 new aircraft have been funded annually, three-quarters of which have been for the battle forces. This compares favourably with the annual average of 254 (73% for the battle force) for the ten years culminating in President Carter's FY79 and FY80 requests for 131 and 123 aircraft respectively. However, procurement of more than 330 aircraft a year would be needed to reach and maintain the force of 7,000 active Navy and Marine Corps aircraft associated with the 600-ship Navy. Faced with the problem of reversing declines in both ship and aircraft inventories simultaneously, the Administration has opted to buy quantities of aircraft already in production to avoid the cost of developing new solutions. In consequence, the fleet will come through the 1990s with aviation capabilities little changed from those of today: the F-14 fighter; F-18 fighter-bomber; A-6, A-7 and AV-8 attack aircraft; E-2C early-warning and EA-6 electronic warfare types; and the S-3A, P-3C and SH-60 anti-submarine warfare aircraft.

So the US Navy can expect to enter the 21st century looking much as it does today: a fleet with a dozen aircraft carrier battle groups as its centrepiece, some 90 to 100 highly capable nuclear-powered attack submarines, 100 frigates, sufficient amphibious ships to lift brigade-size assault forces in each ocean simultaneously, and sufficient seagoing logistics support for sustained operations at great distances from home.

In trying to assess the future of the American fleet it is fairly safe to make the following assumptions:
● US defence strategy and worldwide maritime objectives will change very little.
● The maritime threat posed by the Soviet Union will force the pace and will continue to increase, qualitatively at least.
● The US naval force will grow only modestly, if at all.
● Technological improvements will further transform naval warfare.
● Conflicts short of head-to-head confrontation with the Soviet Union may dictate employment of US naval forces against threats which are sophisticated but less severe than those posed by the Soviets.

Probably the most important trend of the 1980s has been the dispersion of US striking power among platforms other than aircraft carriers. The Tomahawk cruise missile programme, which had to be forced upon the Navy in the mid-1970s, initially produced a 21in-diameter weapon capable of being launched from submarine torpedo tubes. By 1980, however, Tomahawk so matured that US warship designers could contemplate fitting armoured box launchers to destroyers and the four recommissioned battleships, incorporating clusters of vertical launch tubes in destroyers and cruisers, and adding a dozen vertical launch tubes in the bow of *Los Angeles*-class submarines. As a result, the number of ships from which strikes deep into Soviet territory could be launched has now quadrupled – and is due to double again, or even triple, by the turn of the century.

Meanwhile, the pace of the development and fielding of sophisticated conventional weaponry of all kinds has quickened, and ordnance with all-weather capability and increased standoff ranges has been filling the magazines. Attacks on heavily defended targets, afloat or ashore, have become both more likely to succeed and less likely to result in losses to the attacking force. Equally important has been the growing appreciation of the effect that electronic warfare and tactical deception can have on fleet operations.

There has also been an information explosion. Fast-moving technology has made possible the rapid fusion of intelligence data on forces at sea and the aircraft which support them. Naval commanders are now more able than ever to use surveillance information of all kinds to improve tactical readiness and to manoeuvre the fleet so as to maximise the probability of success in the toughest operations.

High technology has also gone a long way towards solving the complex problem of battle management. Nowhere is this more significant than in fleet air defence. Consider the potential threat: waves of a dozen or more long-range bombers, each carrying at least one anti-ship missile, positioned by reconnaissance aircraft and accompanied by electronic warfare support of the most sophisticated kind. In terms of the potential diversity and quantity of the weapons to be dealt with, this is the most urgent threat the carrier battle group faces. Even if the threat sector can be narrowed to 180°, the task of sorting out airborne threats at distances as great as 400 miles – in order to bring bombers under attack before they have reached the weapon-release point – requires enormous effort and co-ordination. A team of four or five E-2Cs and the group's Aegis-configured ships, of which there will be dozens in the fleet at the turn of the century, would play crucial roles in such a battle. They would create the conditions under which an outer air battle could be fought by air-to-air and surface-to-air missiles, greatly reducing the number of bombers and missiles with which the ships of a dispersed battle group would have to contend in the inner zone (within about 100–150 miles) and, subsequently, at terminal or point-defence ranges. Almost overwhelmingly difficult 10–15 years ago, this problem is now well on the way to solution.

Finally, there has been an unmistakable trend towards integration of capabilities across service and theatre lines. Routine deployment of AWACS aircraft to expand the horizon of a carrier battle group; unhesitating provision of land-based tanker aircraft to refuel carrier air wings in flight; integration of overlapping air-defence spheres over land and offshore to achieve regional air superiority: these are prime examples of this joint approach.

If the threat were static, trends like these might justify optimism about America's ability to carry out an aggressive, forward strategy. But Soviet maritime power has not stood still. Instead it has expanded in scope and range as well as in weight.

Most naval experts believe that the Soviet Navy is now unlikely to grow any further. But the capabilities of its ships and aircraft can be expected to improve as new technologies are incorporated. The force is likely to comprise these principal elements over the next 15 years:
● 60-odd ballistic missile submarines
● 125 nuclear and 160 diesel attack submarines
● 8–10 air-capable ships (including at least two small CVNs)
● 110 guided missile cruisers and destroyers
● 180 destroyers and frigates

The anti-air weapon systems and command and control capabilities of the AEGIS-equipped *Ticonderoga* class would be crucial to the outcome of a battle between ASM-carrying bombers and a carrier battle group (*US Navy*)

- 150 small missile combatants
- 150 amphibious ships and transports
- 60 underway replenishment ships and support tankers
- 80 depot and repair ships
- 300 mine countermeasures ships
- 60 intelligence-collecting auxiliaries

A force of about 1,500 land-based naval aircraft (for reconnaissance, anti-submarine warfare, and attack of ships at sea) will support those ships.

How will that large fleet, increasingly capable of operations in the open ocean, be used in the future? It is generally accepted that the Soviet General Staff still sees the principal contribution of the Red Fleet as defence of the homeland. In particular, the fleet is expected to secure areas in which the ballistic missile-armed submarines, the least vulnerable part of the Soviet strategic nuclear force, can operate with impunity. It is also charged with holding at risk the Poseidon, Trident and cruise missile submarines which the US puts to sea, as well as keeping at bay our carrier battle groups and amphibious forces.

The Soviets have optimised their navy in response to the particular strengths of the US fleet, and they continue to do so. Hundreds of Soviet ships and aircraft have been armed with anti-ship (specifically, anti-carrier) missiles. Both diesel and nuclear-powered attack submarines, forming an ever more modern and capable force, are equipped with torpedoes and missiles suitable for attacks on carrier task forces. Soviet anti-submarine warfare training and expertise continue to improve. In the Soviet view these are defensive roles, as are certain specific amphibious tasks in the Baltic Sea and North-west Pacific, and mine warfare functions in some coastal and relatively confined waters.

Depending on the length of a NATO-Warsaw Pact conflict, interdiction of reinforcement and resupply shipping in the Atlantic is almost certainly a Soviet Navy mission. This too is seen as defensive in nature, and is a task for which the huge submarine force is eminently suitable.

Anything the Red Fleet could accomplish beyond these tasks is probably regarded as icing on the cake in the Soviet analysis of how a war with the US would be fought. This means that the more or less permanent peacetime deployment of modest submarine and surface forces to the Mediterranean, South China Sea and Indian Ocean is probably not a harbinger of power projection operations in time of war. These ships perform useful, even highly important show-the-flag and surveillance missions. But the 80-odd ships so deployed would be unsupportable in wartime, lying at the end of long sea lines of communication and having virtually no air cover. They would thus almost certainly be seen as throwaway pieces in a superpower war at sea.

US Navy missions and tasks

Throughout the 1970s US Navy requirements were dictated by four missions: strategic nuclear deterrence, sea control, projection of power ashore, and peacetime presence. More recently, apart from the readiness and security of the sea-based leg of the nuclear triad (the

The threat: Soviet Delta IV-class ballistic missile submarine (above left), the *Kiev*-class carrier *Minsk* (left) and the battle-cruiser *Kirov* (above). (*Royal Norwegian Air Force/Tass*)

ballistic missile submarine force), the naval warfare problem has been seen more as a continuum:
● Forward deployment in peacetime both to deter (by the threat of strike operations) and to stake out a claim to specific sea areas. An important role growing out of this is contingency response.

● Control of selected sea areas (but not entire seas), a prerequisite for strike and amphibious operations and the movement of equipment, troops and supplies by sea.
● Early attack on Soviet strategy and destruction of targets ashore. This is likely to be of greater importance than the engagement of the Red Fleet at sea, although the destruction of Soviet Navy ships at sea is a part of this task.
● Reinforcement and resupply, which, having started well before hostilities commenced, would become

USS *Ohio*, first of the US Navy's latest generation of ballistic missile submarine. (*US Navy*)

logistics system capable of sustaining distant fleet operations for lengthy periods. These back-up functions tie together the principal elements of the fleet – carrier battle forces, attack submarines, ASW and escort forces, amphibious forces – each of which has special strengths in the various areas of combat.

Carrier battle force operations

A carrier battle group (CVBG) consists of an aircraft carrier, about eight surface combatants (four guided missile ships, four ASW ships), and an attack submarine or two in direct support. The carrier's air wing typically consists of some 85 aircraft (24 fighters, ten all-weather bombers, 24 light bombers, four early-warning aircraft, four electronic warfare aircraft, ten fixed-wing ASW aircraft, six ASW/utility helicopters, five tankers). In relation to the demands of a war against the Soviets at sea, the CVBG is but a building block, even though it may be commonly deployed as an entity in peacetime or for contingency operations.

especially critical in the first weeks of the conflict. Control of selected sea areas would be necessary.

This task would be achieved through the successful execution of a familiar set of functions, which would vary in importance depending on geographic location and the weight of the Soviet defence against particular US thrusts: fleet air defence and anti-ship missile defence; anti-submarine warfare, both in broad ocean areas and in immediate defence of a task force or convoy at sea; attack of surface combatants; mining and mine countermeasures; and so on. In support would be extensive ocean surveillance systems, command/control/communications capabilities, and a

Though each US carrier embarks an air group more powerful than many of the world's national air forces, the demands of full-scale war would require these ships to be deployed in battle forces comprising at least three CVBGs. Visible on the deck of USS *John F. Kennedy* are A-6 and A-7 attack aircraft, F-14 fighters, E-2 early-warning aircraft, S-3 anti-submarine aircraft and an ASW/SAR helicopter. (*US Navy*)

Capable of matching the endurance of the nuclear-powered carriers, the *California* and *Virginia*-class cruisers would form a key part of any carrier battle group despatched on a long deployment. Here USS *Virginia, South Carolina, California, Arkansas, Mississippi* and *Texas* form a rare six-ship formation during Exercise READEX 1-81. (*US Navy*)

In sustained combat against the Soviet Navy a carrier battle force – three or more CVBGs combined – would be required for most tasks. This limits the number of simultaneous and separate applications of carrier battle force power to three or four.

Such a force isn't assembled simply to defend itself. It is formed to project power ashore, which means far more than merely hitting naval targets along the coast. In fact, as far as the USSR's objectives and deployments are understood, the deeper inland that strikes from the carriers could reach, the more effect they would have on Soviet strategy. But to do this the carrier battle force would have to penetrate ever denser defences extending 1,500 miles or more to seaward.

As has been the case since shipborne aviation began, the limited volume aboard a carrier must be allocated among aircraft types so that strike and defensive capabilities are balanced. The foremost requirement surveillance and early warning; then there are the principal defensive functions (anti-submarine warfare, fleet air defence, and attack of Soviet battle forces at sea); finally, there must be strike support and bomber aircraft to penetrate defences and destroy the target.

Surveillance is increasingly critical. Using its own resources alone, today's CVBG can see out to a radius of about 400nm. Aircraft, radars, sonars and electronic intercept equipment give the commander a reasonable chance of being alerted to threats – submarine, surface ship and aircraft within that range. This may not however be 360° coverage, but rather is skewed towards the heading along which the force intends to move, or from which the threat is considered most likely to come. Nor is it 100% complete or continuous under even the best circumstances, whatever the range. The battle group commander relies on the Ocean Surveillance Information System (OSIS) to expand his horizon and, to some degree, to incorporate additional information not available from the group's own sensors. If a "threat axis", or sector of high probability of enemy action, can be determined, he may be able to extend the horizon in that direction another 200 miles. If he can do that and bring land-based resources – maritime patrol and AWACS aircraft, electronic interception, over-the-horizon radars – to bear, he may be able to double the extent of his surveillance in certain important respects.

Penetration of the Soviet homeland defence perimeter for either nuclear or conventional operations would without question be the most demanding task imposed on an aircraft carrier battle force. Not to be able to do that would be to abandon large sea areas to the Soviets and to leave key allies to fend for themselves. On the other hand, to do it the Navy must have the most sophisticated, capable and costly weapon systems.

Attacks on Soviet ships at sea would mean dealing with the same quality of threat but, depending on geography, probably not the same density. Aircraft designed to go against homeland targets can quickly be adapted to war at sea; anti-ship weapons with sufficient standoff (ie Harpoon and Tomahawk) enable surface combatants and less sophisticated and capable aircraft to threaten ships as well.

War with the Soviets having been avoided for 40 years, the most frequent employment of carrier battle forces has been relatively short-ranged strike operations against well defended targets under circumstances in which the carriers themselves faced little threat. On average, a half-dozen crises a year since 1945 have prompted deployment or repositioning of carrier battle groups, either to threaten such strike operations or to conduct them. It is hard to imagine that the likelihood of such employment will diminish in the future.

Attack submarine operations

How would a force of 90-plus nuclear-powered attack submarines be best used in a conflict between the US and the Soviet Union? For three decades conventional wisdom has held that, being the most capable of all ASW platforms, SSNs would have to take on the large and diverse Soviet submarine force promptly and decisively, whether in barrier operations far forward, in co-ordinated search-and-destroy operations, in company with carrier battle groups, or on independent patrols. US submarines have been sized, configured and armed primarily for that purpose. Attack of surface ships – the main contribution of US submarines in the last war they fought – has slipped to a distant second in priority. The need to carry some anti-ship ordnance within the limited weapons space of the submarine is grudgingly accepted by the submariners. The fact that the Mk 48 torpedo can do both jobs eases

the problem, but by their very nature the Harpoon and Tomahawk anti-ship missiles must displace anti-submarine weapons. Since destruction of merchant shipping does not loom large as a task in a war with the Soviet Union, and since there are increasing numbers of aircraft and missile systems capable of threatening Soviet warships, the prospect of a major campaign against surface ships has receded for US submariners.

Submariners see the continuing requirement for minelaying as a constraint on the SSN's ability to perform its real mission. Volume taken up by mines is likely to be regarded as space that could have been devoted to more ASW torpedoes. Mine inventories have been maintained, but programmes and training for their actual employment have tended to languish. In fact the Navy has inclined towards the use of Air Force B-52 aircraft for minelaying in forward areas.

What really changes the submarine picture is the advent of the Tomahawk land attack missile (TLAM). Whether fired from a torpedo tube or from vertical launch tubes like those built into the bow of USS *Providence* and subsequent SSNs of the 688 class, TLAM would put the attack submarine at the leading edge of strike operations against the Soviet Union. Submarine-launched TLAMs would be able to strike targets deep inland before they could be reached by even carrier aircraft. Co-ordinated with carrier air strikes, TLAM attacks would significantly increase the effectiveness of strike operations in any conflict, and could well represent the most productive use of the nuclear-powered attack submarine force early in the war.

Surface action group operations

The decision to recommission four battleships with their enormous gun and missile firepower, coupled with the determination to distribute offensive power in the form of Tomahawk missiles among a hundred cruisers and destroyers, revitalised the idea of the surface action group (SAG). This would comprise a battleship, a pair of Aegis-configured cruisers, and other guided missile ships and destroyers, and by definition could operate separately from a carrier battle group. The concept had been attractive to surface warriors, but both lack of credible long-range weaponry and limited capacity for self-defence had militated against the forming of such a force until the renaissance of the battleship.

Now, use of a SAG either within a CVBG (in which case its TLAMs would constitute a major strike potential) or independent of the battle group would make sense in a number of scenarios. All that has been said about the surveillance requirements of a CVBG

The US Navy's quartet of *Iowa*-class battleships, refurbished and fitted with modern electronics and weapon systems, are in many respects the equivalent of the Soviet Navy's *Kirov*-class battlecruisers. Among the new weapon systems visible on USS *Iowa* (above) are the Tomahawk armoured box launchers and white-domed Phalanx close-in anti-aircraft/missile guns, both located amidships. Now superseded as the main armament but still packing a heavyweight punch are the battleships' triple 16in turrets (right). (*US Navy*)

would apply to SAG operations, except that organic surveillance capabilities would be significantly shorter-ranged than those provided by carrier aircraft, and expansion of the surveillance horizon would be all the more critical.

Amphibious operations

At present the US Navy only has enough amphibious shipping to lift one of the four existing Marine division-size forces for an assault (and that, because the ships are split between Atlantic and Pacific Fleets, would take months of preparation and shifting of forces). This is far below the stated requirement for three divisions to successfully assault a well defended amphibious objective area. In fact current amphibious assault capability is more like a heavy brigade (upwards of 15,000 Marines) in each ocean simultaneously. When the 600-ship Navy is achieved in the early 1990s that capability may have been improved to "a MAF and a MAB" – a division and its air wing in one ocean and a brigade-sized effort in the other – depending on how much time is available to assemble the necessary shipping.

However, an important outcome of Rapid Deployment Force planning in the late 1970s has been the acquisition of maritime prepositioned ships (MPS)

Two generations of US Navy amphibious assault ship: USS *Guam* (top) and *Wasp* (above). **The latter, first of its class, is due to commission in 1989.**

and the development of imaginative concepts for their employment. While not actually an assault capability, the MPS programme makes possible efficient ship-to-shore movement of Marines in a way which would clearly add to assault capabilities. Large roll-on/roll-off ships, four of which are capable of prepositioning forward a brigade's unit equipment and holding supplies in near-ready dehumidified storage, together with airlifting of a ready brigade of Marines to marry up with the prepositioned equipment, make it possible to put a division-size force ashore once brigade and equipment have been married up. At the time of writing there is a brigade set of equipment in the Indian Ocean and another ready for deployment to the Eastern Atlantic, with brigades already designated and trained for prompt airlift to the scene of the action.

Whether a future amphibious operation were to be pure assault or some combination of assault and MPS, the requirement for air superiority and offshore support would almost certainly mean commitment of a carrier battle force until the landing force could be well established ashore. Surveillance, communications and logistics would be identical with those of the battle force for some time (days or weeks) until the objective area was reasonably secure and Marine aviation capabilities – fighters, bombers, electronic warfare aircraft, helicopters – were in place. When the carrier battle force then moved on, airborne early warning, battle management and ELINT/COMINT requirements, little diminished, would devolve to forces ashore.

Defence of merchant shipping

National strategy calls for timely reinforcement of NATO and sustained resupply of allied forces engaged in combat in Europe. More than 90% of this logistic effort would be seaborne. If the NATO nations acted on strategic warning, it might well begin well before conflict is joined. For a war lasting more than a few days, seaborne logistics would be crucial to the repelling the Warsaw Pact advance and success along the Central Front. The Soviets certainly recognise this: the proportion of their maritime forces devoted to interdiction of reinforcement/resupply would be indicative of how good they estimated NATO's staying power to be.

Three generations of US Navy escort: USS *Knox*, lead ship of the *Knox* class of frigates (above right); ***Nicholson*, a *Spruance*-class destroyer** (right); **and an artist's impression of *Arleigh Burke*, first of the USN's latest destroyer class** (overleaf). **(*US Navy*)**

In any event, NATO would have to marshal merchant shipping of all kinds (as many as 1,000 nationally controlled ships and as many others as could be commandeered), empty it of peacetime cargo and send it across the Atlantic. Newer, faster ships could be expected to sail independently or in small groups; slower ships, comprising two-thirds of the total, would undoubtedly sail in convoys. Routing and protection of this flow of ships would be SACLANT's major concern. It is likely that a "zone defence" would have to be adopted to make the most efficient use of the ASW forces available.

Individual NATO nations maintain some 400 ASW frigates and destroyers in readiness for convoy protection, along with 300 long-range maritime patrol aircraft. The US contribution is roughly one-third of the destroyers and frigates and more than half of the maritime patrol aviation. But the Allied total is far less than what conservative analysis indicates the requirement to be. An even more critical deficiency is the general lack of resources with which to gain air superiority and so enable these ASW forces to operate. Unless the US devotes aircraft carriers to the task, large areas of the Atlantic could be subject to Soviet air attack. Improved surveillance, judicious use of NATO's smaller aircraft carriers and land bases, and more widely distributed point defences would be required to make critical transoceanic routes safe.

Prospects

Someone said that making predictions is hard – especially when one is dealing with the future. The present momentum in strategy, investment and force employment will carry the US Navy into the 21st century with few surprises. The decisions which shape the future of a navy are those which deal with today's allocation of resources between the size and character of the force structure, the rate at which new technologies are applied to modernisation of existing systems, the readiness for combat of the force in being, and the degree of sustainability of that force in the face of wartime consumption rates. Force employment options are as much a function of the above as of what the world situation or the enemy's actions might be. By their individual actions on force structure and modernisation, the Soviet Union and the United States have largely defined the nature of maritime confrontations between them for decades to come; the outcome of conflict at sea would largely depend on the readiness of the opposing forces, and how long operations at sea could be sustained.

Resource allocation tends to run in cycles, on the US side at least. After determined investment in force structure and modernisation for several years, it is inevitable that the emphasis will shift in the not too distant future to improved readiness and greater sustainability – which suggests investment in weaponry rather than platforms, in people rather than in hardware, in logistics rather than in development of new systems.

Nevertheless, some changes in the character of the force structure are predictable. Now that a force of a dozen or more big aircraft carriers is assured, there will be renewed pressure to diversify aviation-capable platforms even further. Amphibious flight decks – LPHs, LHAs, LHDs – are already due to come into the force in larger numbers. Recognised as flexible, multi-purpose platforms from which helicopters, AV-8s and tilt-rotors can be flown for a variety of purposes, these ships will become even more important. Even as LAMPS III (SH-60) helicopters arrive in the force in significant numbers, the operational demand for still more far-reaching ASW, AEW and ELINT/COMINT aviation capabilities for surface combatants is generating a requirement for more dispersed decks. Whatever the new frigate (FFX) turns out to be, it will almost certainly have air capabilities vastly better than those of today's frigates, destroyers and cruisers. The ARAPAHO concept – adaptation of a container ship to embark and operate ASW helicopters in addition to (on top of) its cargo – may well evoke new interest. The smaller carrier designs of the early 1970s may even be reconsidered, in view of the need both to move the surveillance horizon outwards (farther out than aircraft launched from a large carrier at the centre of the battle force can manage) and to allocate less carrier deck space to support functions. Moreover, the US needs red chips as well as blue chips – options smaller than full-blown carrier battle groups – with which to play for its maritime objectives.

Attack submarine operations will have to become less independent and more integrated with what the fleet is doing as a whole. SSN capabilities in strike warfare, anti-surface operations and mining will undoubtedly become as important in many scenarios as their ASW prowess.

The advent of stealth – or, more specifically, the raising of the collective consciousness of the observability of ships, aircraft and weapons – will demand high-technology solutions to detection, tracking and terminal homing problems and will slowly but surely influence the design and operation of most of the systems the US Navy puts to sea.

Standoff distances and the autonomy of weapons used at sea or for attack of targets ashore will have to

increase in view of the proliferation of effective air defences, both Soviet and Third World.

"Battle management" systems will become more and more powerful as surveillance and tactical data exchange are improved and expert systems ("artificial intelligence") are widely applied to warfare at sea.

These changes will of course have implications for the numbers, intelligence and skills of the sailors who man the Navy's ships and aircraft. There will be both pluses and minuses as new systems become operational. Nevertheless, manning of the fleet will be the subject of continuing concern and debate for the next few years as the nation moves into a projected "valley" in the population of 18-year-olds eligible for military service. Because so many of the constraints involved are matters of policy and economics, it is safe to predict that, one way or another, the United States will find enough qualified and motivated people to do the job.

Attack submarine USS *Houston* (SSN-713). Currently tasked with the hunting and destruction of enemy submarines, these boats will increasingly take on extra roles, including mine warfare and anti-surface operations. (*US Navy*)

Budget pressures threaten British amphibious fleet

First published in *Jane's Defence Weekly*.

Joseph Porter

HMS *Intrepid*, one of Britain's two ageing amphibious assault ships. (*Mike Lennon*)

One of the major decisions facing the British Ministry of Defence is whether to replace its ageing amphibious fleet, of which the key ships are *Fearless* and *Intrepid*. Yet there seem to be few topics which Government defence spokesmen are less willing to discuss. Having in his 1985 Statement of Defence Estimates described the NATO Northern Flank as "of vital importance," former Defence Secretary Michael Heseltine then told the House of Commons Defence Committee of a need to delay any decision on the new amphibious ships for as long as possible, probably until the middle of 1986. Such procrastination has been a continued source of irritation to the Defence Committee.

The debate about the future amphibious ships turns on the NATO Northern Flank, with operations outside the NATO area important but subsidiary. This is an area of defence policy in which the major British political parties show a notable unanimity of anxiety.

They are not alone. US Secretary of the Navy John Lehman is "extremely worried" that the Royal Marine force may lose its amphibious shipping. Supreme Allied Commander Atlantic Adm Wesley McDonald said last year: "The US, of course, continues to build its amphibious forces. I'd like to believe that the Royal Navy will continue, although it's a tough decision on priorities on how you spend the money." And the House of Commons Defence Committee, reporting on May 23, 1985, was unequivocal: "If the United Kingdom does not replace its amphibious capability, NATO's reinforcement plans for the Northern Flank will be in jeopardy."

Away from the political arena, the indications are that the British military are agreed on the need to preserve the nation's amphibious capability. There is an air of a tumultuous debate concluded within the MoD, and the sound of departments falling in line behind the decision.

Analysing reinforcement and intervention operations in 1960, the respected military historian Sir Basil Liddell Hart expressed a view that many see as still valid: "On a superficial view, airborne forces may appear to be a better counter, as being quicker to arrive. But their strategic movement, and effect on arrival, are subject to many limitations. . . . In tackling emergencies, two hands are better than one – and essential when one is unreliable. While it is desirable to have an airborne force which enables quicker intervention where it is possible, it is essential to have a marine force, and better that this should be the bigger of the two. The use of an airborne force, or of any land-based force, is a more irrevocable step, since its commitment is more definite and its withdrawal more difficult. A self-contained and sea-based amphibious force, of which the US Marine Corps is the prototype, is the best kind of fire extinguisher because of its flexibility, reliability, logistic simplicity and relative economy."

The Falklands War did much to remind the UK of the realities of worldwide peacekeeping and deterrent operations. On November 29, 1983, Minister of State John Stanley said that the campaign had "also demonstrated the immense value of HMS *Fearless* and HMS *Intrepid* in launching and supporting amphibious

The United States has no doubts about the value of an amphibious assault capability: the *Austin*-class amphibious transport dock *Nashville* (below) is comparable with the British *Fearless* and *Intrepid*; at least 14 dock landing ships of the *Whidbey Island* class (inset) are to be built. (*Wright & Logan/US Navy*)

The "immensely valuable" HMS *Intrepid*. (*Wright & Logan*)

operations". The operation was of necessity essentially maritime. The distances would have been daunting for air reinforcement at the best of times, but by 1982 RAF Support Command had been permitted to decline to a level where nothing of the kind could have been contemplated.

Remedies are in fact now in hand, with the improvements to the British Army Airborne Brigade's capacity for operations outside the NATO area reported to be nearly complete, and a commitment to an air reinforcement re-equipment programme, including the introduction of wide-bodied transports. But this preoccupation with the air, to the apparent exclusion of sealift, suggests that the British Government believes the peacekeeping job can be done on the cheap by airlift alone. Or could it be that, for once, economic considerations are outweighed by military prejudices? One such, also a result of Falklands experiences, is the supposed vulnerability of ships. In the USA the argument has been disposed of summarily by Navy Secretary Lehman, who has questioned the logic that holds that ships steaming at 30kt are vulnerable, while stockpiles moving at zero knots and placed nearer the enemy are not.

British naval apologists point out that the Royal Navy's ships in the Falklands, which were certainly not optimised for inshore anti-air warfare, formed the bulk of the forces opposing the only truly effective

This – and worse – is what happens when air defence fails a seaborne assault force. The since repaired logistic landing ship *Sir Tristram* pictured at Port Stanley in 1982. (*L. & L. van Ginderen*)

Argentinian element, the air force. But this was fought to a standstill over San Carlos without any loss to its main target, the main assault landing force in the amphibious ships. The US Navy considers that at that time the British escorts were deficient in anti-air armament, and the marked subsequent improvements are viewed with approval.

Vulnerable or not, ships have one major advantage over aircraft when it comes to moving masses of stores, equipment and troops. The point has been made nicely in the House of Commons by Jarrow member Don

Dixon. If a horse emulated Pegasus and grew wings, he said, it might be able to lift about 15lb (7kg) of books off the table in front of him. If, on the other hand, it preferred to swim, it could probably tow 50 or 60 Honourable Members through the sea. Specifically, one horsepower can move 15lb by air, but 9,000lb by sea.

In the article cited earlier, Liddell Hart pointed out some of airlift's other drawbacks: "Strategic movement by air is so liable to be blocked or impeded by countries in its path that it is becoming strategically unreliable as a way of meeting the worldwide problems of the Atlantic Alliance. . . . Moreover, on arrival, an airborne force needs airfields for its disembarkation and logistic support. Adequate ones for large aircraft and a large force do not exist in many areas, and even when they do they may be in hostile hands. If well defended, an attempt to capture them by parachute drop can easily turn into disaster, while a ground approach may be checked through lack of tactical mobility and of weapon power to overcome strong resistance. For an airborne force is narrowly limited in the vehicles, heavy weapons and ammunition it can carry. If it is held up and has to wait for these requirements to arrive by sea,

Argentinian Mirage overflies a British logistic landing ship during the Falklands War. Though operating in unfavourable circumstances and deficient in anti-air weaponry, the Royal Navy fought the Argentinian Air Force to a standstill without loss to the main amphibious assault force. (*Royal Navy*)

it loses its main advantage, rapidity of intervention. Another of its drawbacks is its vulnerability to intercept while in transit."

He might also have mentioned the weather, which is a major limitation on aircraft operations in northern Norway, and the problems of resupplying airborne forces once landed.

Northern Norway, which borders the USSR, is a likely and very challenging arena for British and Dutch light mobile reinforcement operations in time of tension between the Warsaw Pact and NATO. Norway has three major characteristics in the eyes of the military planner: its size and shortage of internal communications; its Arctic climate; and its place in what is called the "Nordic balance". To preserve the last Norway refuses to accept permanent stationing of other NATO countries' troops on its soil, although periodic exercises and the stockpiling of stores and munitions (some hundreds of miles from likely battle areas) are encouraged.

Next, Norway's mountainous terrain makes massed land-mobile operations impracticable. The only complete north-south surface link is a two-lane road, supplemented by a railway for part of the distance. But ports and airfields are not plentiful, although the coast has many deep fjords, some of which run to within a few kilometres of the Swedish and Finnish borders. Taken together, these factors mean that it is as difficult to move large quantities of military equipment within Norway as it would be to bring supplies in from other NATO European countries.

Finally there is Norway's Arctic climate. Though in winter many areas are more passable than they are in summer, when the valleys tend to be soft going, only specialist Arctic-trained troops can cope with the extreme cold. A total of five Norwegian national brigades are at short notice to take up positions in the north.

Other significant reinforcements for the Northern Flank are the three/four battalion UK/Netherlands Amphibious Force (UKNL AF), the Canadian Air-Sea Transportable (CAST) Brigade, the Allied Command Europe's Mobile Force, and elements of a US Marine Corps amphibious brigade.

Of these, the UKNL AF is reported to be substantially the best trained for the task and is likely to be the first to arrive fully ready in the battle area. Moreover, it carries all its own stores, ammunition, artillery and air defence, and also has its own sea and airlift; it is unique in being entirely self-contained and independent of host-nation support.

What could small formations like UKNL AF do against an invading Soviet force of several divisions? In fact the odds are not as bad as they look: the Norwegian terrain generally favours the established defender, while the same factors that complicate the NATO defensive deployment also constrain the

An *Invincible*-class carrier could perform a "quick dash" with a Royal Marine commando to supplement an amphibious force. HMS *Invincible* seen off Norway in spring 1985. (*Royal Navy*)

would-be invader. Thus, as with the Germans in Italy in 1944, smaller numbers of well placed and resolute troops could hold an attack. The airborne threat is more of a problem, however. The Soviets could, it is believed, rapidly concentrate 400 close air support (CAS) aircraft, 100 attack helicopters and, a new worry, 200 utility helicopters. There is also a substantial amphibious force and the means to paradrop an airborne division. All this must be countered by NATO air forces, which could in the event include the USMC interceptor squadrons and the USN aircraft in the attack carriers. Favouring this defensive effort would be the fact that, initially at least, the Soviet air forces would be operating at long ranges comparable with those which so limited the Argentinians in the Falklands War.

The keystone to a successful defence in Norway would be prompt reinforcement. The Soviets themselves would need a few days to deploy forces into the Kola Peninsula and bring them to their full potential. Early action, apart from underlining NATO's resolution, would also increase the reinforcements' chances of getting to their battle positions unscathed. Delay, on the other hand, could expose NATO amphibious forces to attack at sea, and invite a pre-emptive strike on the host-nation infrastructure, including the strategic airfields.

There is certainly a strong case for moving the advance element of the UKNL AF by air. But to try to insert it all by this means would be quite another matter, there being only five substantial airheads in the relevant area of northern Norway: Bodo, Tromso, Andoya, Bardufoss and Evenes. In addition to providing for NATO air defence long-range maritime patrol aircraft, they would have to cope with the bulk of the Norwegian Army troops deploying north and with advance elements of the CAST Brigade and the USMC. Quite apart from the resulting congestion and the possible lack of host-nation transportation forward to battle areas, it would surely be unhealthy to add to such vulnerable concentrations.

Moreover, getting the full UKNL AF to Norway, probably with only very light scales of ammunition and without most of its supporting arms, would require 500 C-130 Hercules sorties. This looks scarcely practicable in view of all the other calls likely to be made on RAF Support Command. Nor could an airlift of this magnitude be instantaneous. Instead it would extend over several days, and then the heavy equipment would have to follow by sea anyway. Assuming that it takes as long to assemble troops at airheads as at embarkation ports, this would all seem to cancel out the time-saving advantages of airlift, since the sea passage would take only three or five days (depending on whether the sailing was from the north or the south of the UK).

The advantages of transporting the UKNL reinforce-

ment as a whole and maintaining its complete independence of host-nation support are substantial. For one, it would arrive in the battle area with all it needed to fight. Further, ordering an amphibious force to set sail for an unspecified destination might well be an easier political decision than the despatch of air reinforcement; an amphibious force need not be committed to any particular battle area until the moment that troops begin to land.

Liddell Hart points out that this latter characteristic gives the force deterrent capability in excess of its normal strength, since the enemy will be uncertain up to the last minute of where it will actually be inserted, and will therefore be kept disproportionately off balance. This is both politically and militarily desirable, particularly as the force can be held offshore for a prolonged period. Once the force has been landed, the ships can continue to multiply its effect by lying in wait as a ready means of redeployment, or by providing command and control facilities.

On the question of vulnerability, airfields must be at least as open to attack as Secretary Lehman's static stockpiles. And though it is true that bombed airfields do not sink, the aircraft, troops and equipment destroyed at the same time cannot readily be replaced, however efficiently the holes in the runways are filled.

Though the hasty taking up and modification of commercial shipping worked well in the Falklands War, the sheer speed of events in any future European conflict would probably rule out this solution to the problem of transporting Northern Flank reinforcements. Here the North Sea ferry *Norland* is fitted with a helicopter deck before sailing for the South Atlantic.

Mobility is one way of protecting ships. Good air defence is another, and in this respect the RN is in the lead amongst European NATO navies. The UKNL AF might also be protected also by elements of the strike fleet, or by combat-proven Sea Harriers from the *Invincible*-class light carriers. The latter would be confronted by a hard but not impossible task, particularly now that the carriers have embarked AEW, for even if the Soviets could concentrate their full close air support effort exclusively on the UKNL AF, the rate of strike aircraft sorties might not be more than about twice that achieved by the Argentinians.

No amphibious commander wants to assault a prepared defensive position directly from the sea. To avoid this necessity he is usually able to achieve tactical surprise and land on unoccupied ground of his choosing. This is not the same thing as seeking always to land in a non-military manner, using dockside

facilities. Such an aim in Norway is in any case unrealistic, the ports there are subject to most of the constraints affecting the airheads. Instead there is great scope for amphibious methods as a result of the wide availability of suitable beaches and helicopter landing zones. Compared with the sparse fixed installations, these sites offer far greater flexibility.

The arguments for NATO amphibious capability also hold good for unilateral peacekeeping operations, whether within the alliance area or beyond it. In fact the great majority of operations by British forces since the Second World War have taken place outside the NATO area.

Nations such as Britain and France, which subscribe to NATO while retaining a worldwide strategic perspective and sense of responsibility, must configure their limited military resources for as wide a range of applications as possible, within or beyond the NATO area. Perpetuation of the UK's amphibious force is

essential to the maintenance of such a long range intervention capability.

The Commons Defence Committee fears that financial considerations will outweigh military ones when it finally comes to a decision on the amphibious ships. But by comparison with other major defence programmes, the successors to *Intrepid* and *Fearless* would be cheap indeed. A pair of ships to similar but updated US Navy designs could be built in UK yards for between £500 million and £1,000 million. This is well below the cost of programmes such as Tornado, Trident, the main battle tank replacement, and the European Fighter Aircraft.

Left: **Operating Sea Harriers from *Invincible*-class light carriers, the Royal Navy could give adequate air cover to an amphibious assault force in Norwegian waters.**

Below: **EAP, forerunner of the European Fighter Aircraft. Programmes like this will cost many times more than a pair of new assault ships. (*BAe*)**

The Indian Ocean's uneasy rim

Capt John Moore RN

One of the prime causes of anxiety in the foreign ministries of the non-communist world is the condition known as "instability". Resulting from divisions within a country, differences between countries, or imbalances in various forms of armaments, this state of affairs currently prevails in an increasing number of areas around the world. The largest concentration of such potential trouble spots is in the zone surrounding the Indian Ocean, a region of which the average Westerner is largely ignorant. And since the voter is in theory at least the curb on ill-advised political acts in the West, his lack of knowledge of the motives and attitudes of these nations can only make a difficult situation worse. All the main races and religions of the world are represented in these nations, and their cultures vary from the primitive to the most sophisticated. The speedy dismemberment of the

India possesses by far the most powerful navy in the Indian Ocean region. It operates a mix of Soviet and Western equipment, including the Nanuchka II-class missile corvette *Vijay Durg*.

European empires following the Second World War turned the area into a patchwork of states, all industrially underdeveloped and therefore dependent on external aid. Such assistance has rarely come without political strings attached.

There is also a general lack of understanding of the maritime factors affecting this huge area, which is centred on the third largest in the world. Distances are vast: from South Africa to Australia is twice as far as from Great Britain to Canada, and transoceanic passages are rarely less than 4,000 miles. Exit and entry points are few and, in the north, extremely confined. Thus the very large volume of merchant shipping needed to sustain not only the countries bordering the ocean but also the majority of the region's non-communist states is concentrated in very small stretches of water and is therefore very vulnerable to attack by any one of half a dozen methods.

The monsoonal climate of the northern part of the Indian Ocean can have profound effects on shipping operations. The weather varies far more than in temperate areas, from flat calm to winds of hurricane force. The effects of such a diversity of naval operations will be discussed later.

But of all the influences on the naval situation in the Indian Ocean, the most significant recently has been the action of foreign powers. Any naval review of this region must therefore start with the external forces at work before moving to the indigenous navies and, lastly, the possibility of collisions between the two.

With the final withdrawal of the main bulk of British forces from East of Suez in the late 1960s, 200 years of direct influence on affairs came to an end. Of the two powers to emerge from the Second World War with enough strength to act as international arbiters, the USSR had a national aim of expansion while the USA, with a more peaceful approach, was forced into reactive policies. The Vietnam War may have been a

reaction to a phantom Chinese threat but the results – the weakening of American influence, the undermining of American purpose and the Nixon doctrine of non-interference ashore, except by means of aid – had a real effect on the advancement of Soviet foreign policy. The first tentative Soviet naval moves into the Indian Ocean coincided with the start of the war, and the subsequent policy of détente between West and East benefited the Kremlin through the euphemistically termed "correlation of forces". Throughout this period the Russians were busily making friends and influencing people wherever they found a national door slightly ajar.

In 1977 Soviet forces were asked to leave Somalia as the USSR's support for Ethiopia made itself plain, culminating in the great airlift of 1977–78. At the same time, support for Vietnam's invasion of Cambodia ensured a Soviet lodgement in the old American bases of Da Nang and Cam Ranh Bay. The sequence of aid, civilian advisers, military advisers, military hardware and treaties of friendship led again and again to the acquisition of base facilities. To date this tireless effort has yielded facilities in Cuba, Angola, Mozambique, Ethiopia, Aden and Vietnam. There have been failures in Iraq and Somalia, but in the Indian Ocean anchorages have been established off the Seychelles and support agreements concluded with Mauritius. And in addition to this overt effort, every Soviet ship, be it a space tracking vessel or a fishing trawler, must be considered as part of a gigantic maritime capability.

Although the USA had long maintained a small naval force in the Gulf and Arabian Sea area, it was not until 1979 that a permanent, large-scale fleet was

Typical of the Soviet vessels to be found routinely in the Indian Ocean is the space research ship *Akademik Sergei Korolev*. (*Mike Lennon*)

sent to the Indian Ocean. With the Anglo-American agreement providing a base at Diego Garcia, the Rapid Deployment Force was speedily assembled and sent to that island. Otherwise 1979 was not a happy year for the USA in the Indian Ocean. The expulsion of the Shah of Iran and the subsequent chaos in that country not only removed a friendly state from the US orbit but also encouraged the Soviet invasion of Afghanistan that December.

Thus by early 1980 the situation was far from encouraging. The USA had no diplomatic links with Iraq, had lost her foothold in Iran and had the Tehran hostage crisis to resolve. Her ambassador to Afghanistan had been murdered in the previous year, while relations with Pakistan and India were at a low ebb. In April the hostages were released. In September the Iran-Iraq war began. In November Ronald Reagan was elected President of the USA and inherited, amongst many other problems, the question of the future of the American bases in the Philippines. The naval base at Subic Bay and the air base at Clark Field are essential to the maintenance of American forces in the Indian Ocean. The current

bilateral agreement on their use does not expire until 1991, but until new President Corazon Aquino has consolidated her grip on power, doubts about this arrangement must persist. No alternative facilities exist within 1,500 miles.

Other ports of call for the US fleet are strung around the ocean's periphery, and none can dock and service large warships. The French have access to the facilities of Djibouti for their squadron and also maintain small land and air forces there. British ships detached to the Gulf area can dock at Mombasa. The US Navy visits Karachi, but the facilities there are inadequate for large and highly sophisticated ships and the same is true of Cockburn Sound in Western Australia. Singapore has huge docks but the naval element in Sembawang has drained away. Finally, the search for alternative havens is bedevilled by the difficulty of persuading small countries to cast in their lot with one of the superpowers in an area where many nations seek to remain uncommitted.

Of the littoral states only one, India, has a fleet of any proportions. At one time Australia's fleet approached the Indian Navy in capability, but the loss

Two of the most professional navies in the region are enjoying widely different fortunes at present. The Indian Navy, represented here by the frigate *Dunagiri* (above), is expanding rapidly. The Australian fleet, by contrast, can't afford to put helicopters aboard HMAS *Canberra* (below) and her three FFG-7-class sisters. (*Graeme K. Andrews Productions*)

Malaysian *Spica*-class fast attack craft. (*Bofors*)

of its single aircraft carrier and the current lack of
anti-submarine helicopters for the four FFG-7 frigates
has markedly reduced its capabilities. Australia's
naval strength is now insufficient to permit any
concentration of effort in the deep field if there are
simultaneous requirements on her northern and
eastern seaboards. The navies of Indonesia, Malaysia
and Singapore comprise, with the exception of the few
frigates belonging to the first two, ships and craft
designed primarily for operations in coastal waters.
These three navies are however well armed with
missile craft which could contest the passage of the
Malacca Straits. (See *South-east Asia: a key alliance
under pressure* for a full review of the navies of
Australia and the ASEAN nations.)

Burma's problems are primarily internal and her
navy is with very few exceptions elderly and tasked
with coastal and river patrols. The economy is in severe
decline under the leadership of the 75-year-old Ne
Win. A high proportion of the 179,000 members of
the armed forces are engaged in a constant war with
various ethnic rebel groups, such as the Shans and
Mons entrenched on the northern and eastern
frontiers. Although aid from Australia, Britain,
China, West Germany, Japan, Malaysia, the USA and

Carpentaria-class fishery protection vessel of the Burmese
Navy. (*Graeme K. Andrews Productions*)

Yugoslavia is mainly directed towards agriculture,
development of the huge reserves of natural gas
discovered 100 miles offshore in the Gulf of Martaban
would force a radical change. Like many of the littoral
countries Burma suffers from a chronic energy
shortage, and the gas would go far towards alleviating

Top: **Shanghai-class patrol boats of the Bangladeshi Navy.** (*Graeme K. Andrews Productions*)

Above: *Babur* **(ex-HMS** *London*), **flagship of the Pakistani Navy.** (*Mike Lennon*)

this. But foreign capital, technical aid and shipbuilding would be needed, calling for a reversal of the isolationist policies followed by Ne Win since he took power in 1962.

The brief war between India, supported by the Soviet Union, and Pakistan, with very lukewarm backing from the USA and China, which resulted in the creation of Bangladesh from what was previously East Pakistan left the new nation defenceless on the water. The succeeding 15 years have seen the creation of a useful fleet with, as its core, three elderly British frigates; a large force of light craft, including four Chinese missile craft; and 28 other vessels, ranging from 400-ton Chinese craft to a class of five river patrol craft built at Dhaka. A small afloat support force and two floating docks complete a small navy well adapted to the needs of a country with a coastline of only 350 miles but a huge riverine system amongst the Sundarbans. The main bases are at Chittagong and Khulna, the latter being the focus for river patrol work.

The Sri Lankan authorities have no such bases in the north of their country, where the navy is engaged in patrols against Tamil infiltrators and illegal immigrants from southern India. The Palk Strait, centre of these operations, bristles with navigational hazards, and the six merchant ships converted as surveillance command ships are probably proving a sound investment. Most of the craft that they support are locally built at Colombo Dockyard and range from 21 to 330 tons displacement. None is heavily armed, the biggest guns in the navy being the 37mm weapons in the six Chinese Shanghai-class fast attack craft. Though this is little more than a coastguard force, the magnificent harbour of Trincomalee, on the east coast of Sri Lanka, remains free of foreign interference despite its immensely important strategic position.

Pakistan's one main harbour, at Karachi, doubles as a naval base and the centre for all overseas trade. It is also the centre for local industry and the sole oil-importing point. With a total coastline of only 650 miles to police, much of which lies within the boundaries of inhospitable Baluchistan, the navy has no doubts about its role: the defence of trade and the prevention of interference with the shore side of that trade by hostile amphibious operations. Aggressive operations by the Pakistani Navy reduce its ability to perform this vital role, and anyway the fleet is not fitted for such action. The six French-built submarines are barely numerous enough for long-range surveillance and defence deployments, while the main surface force of one British County-class light cruiser and six ex-USN destroyers is too small to form effective sub-units. Eight Chinese missile craft and 16 fast attack craft complete the line-up of front-line combatant ships. A number of auxiliaries will need replacement in the near future and the minuscule MCM force of three ships is well overdue for modernisation.

Pakistan is not a rich country, however, and the government tends to favour the land-based forces. This is not surprising now that Soviet forces in Afghanistan are operating within a few hours' bus ride of Peshawar, while the eastern frontier with India stretches for some 1,000 miles from the Karakorams to the sea. Nonetheless, the essential need is to maintain the exclusively maritime supply routes from the south. Though this situation is acknowledged in the current plans to build three frigates, such a small programme should be only a beginning. The weather conditions off the coast are highly variable, making anti-submarine operations very complex. Helicopters and towed arrays, in both warships and auxiliaries, could assist in these tasks. At the same time there is a pressing need for a core of modern front-line ships at the lowest possible cost.

In an area of extreme uncertainty dependence on seaborne trade is a major liability. Pakistan has to import most of her oil, has some natural gas reserves, and derives a small amount of hydro-electric power from two major dams. This precarious position could have been avoided if Pakistan had been granted timely access to US nuclear power station technology, but continued opposition in Congress long delayed such a move. While the USA was prepared to transfer warships to protect the oil imports, nuclear proliferation fears ruled out a step which would have ameliorated the situation.

Pakistan is a Muslim state, her connections with Saudi Arabia are close, and she is on good terms with the other Gulf states. Officers from the navies of Iran, Iraq, Saudi Arabia, the UAE and Oman are currently being trained in Karachi. Though this should not be seen as a major maritime alliance in the making, it certainly suggests a community of interest.

Maritime affairs in the Gulf are dominated by the long-running war between Iran and Iraq. While the conflict's land operations affect the two protagonists alone, the continuing attacks on merchant shipping give it an international dimension. Ships have been attacked both inside and outside the declared zones, though vessels sailing by night and lying up by day have been immune. Although a number have been struck by Exocet missiles launched from Iraqi aircraft, the results have been patchy. The main danger has been fire, but relatively few of the ships attacked have been declared constructive total losses. The Iranian use of television-guided Maverick weapons has not been a success, while rocket and machine gun fire has resulted in handfuls of casualties. The impression is that concentrated attacks from the beginning on oil terminals such as Kharg Island would have yielded better returns.

The war is taking place in a zone which has wider interest for both the Soviet Union and the Western powers. From Turkey through Israel to Egypt, from Pakistan to the Horn of Africa, the area is criss-crossed with military and economic relationships. At present the major powers remain outside the Gulf, while the link between Iraq and South Yemen has been strained to breaking point, the threat to Oman from South Yemen has been averted, and the Arab Gulf states have created the Gulf Co-operation Council. This grouping may well be intended as a means of co-ordinating action against threats stemming from

rapid modernisation, the presence of large numbers of foreigners in the various states, or disaffection amongst Shia minorities influenced by the Iranian brand of fundamentalism.

At a time when the OPEC grip on Western economies has diminished and the Gulf rulers are concerned over their future, the local forces are far more land-based than maritime. Only Saudi Arabia, with coastlines in both the Gulf and the Red Sea, has opted for frigate-sized ships and afloat support. Four French-built frigates and over a dozen missile craft, two dozen hovercraft and some 50 patrol craft are backed by a coastguard with 450 craft ranging in size from three tons to 350. Preventing infiltration on these barren coasts is a huge task, made harder by the fact that the small Gulf states have correspondingly small navies. But the majority of the craft are modern and many are equipped with missiles.

Oman, at the entrance to the Gulf, has an interesting and fairly typical mix of ships: missile and gun boats, inshore patrol craft, landing ships and craft, and a sizeable number of police vessels. Beyond the Strait of Hormuz the big-power navies spend long periods at

Deadly adversaries in the Gulf War, Iran and Iraq both entered the conflict with well balanced naval forces. Iran's dozen-strong force of *Kaman*-class (French *La Combattante II*) fast attack craft, represented here by *Shamir* (top), is reported to have shrunk to eight as a result of losses in combat. Iran's quartet of Polish-built Polnochny-class landing ships – this is *Ganda* (above), second to be delivered – has suffered a single loss.

sea, although the Soviet squadron has two bases reasonably close at hand in Aden and the Dahlak Islands off Ethiopia. South Yemen, with its capital at Aden, is the only Marxist Arab state. The Soviets have a firm emplacement there, though their representatives are not beloved of the local population. At the same time the policies and actions of the Aden government have not been entirely doctinaire: the treaties of friendship with the USSR and Ethiopia in 1978 and 1979 have been balanced by the border war with North Yemen in 1979 and attempts since 1980 to improve relations with the Gulf states. Yet despite these apparent inconsistencies South Yemen is unlikely

The Saudi Arabian replenishment ship *Boraida*, one of a pair of modified *Durance*-class vessels supplied by France. (*L. & L. van Ginderen*)

to drift from the Soviet side, and its small navy continues to rely on supplies from the USSR. The tiny fleet of North Yemen is similarly dependent, while that of Ethiopia has been built up by Soviet transfers of two frigates, two landing craft, four missile craft and several patrol craft. This was the small price paid for the use of the facilities on the Dahlak Islands, with their three docks and shore workshops and accommodation.

The nearest Western base in the area is the facility at Djibouti used by the French squadron. The US fleet would find the use of Berbera in Somalia, until 1977 an important Soviet haven, politically difficult if good relations were to be maintained with Kenya, keystone of America's African policy. Complicating the matter is Somalia's persistent claim to sections of Kenya's northern territory. The issue may however be settled by Kenya's rocky financial condition, which demands continuing accord with Western countries. The military facilities enjoyed by both the British and Americans are also an indication of Kenyan tacit support for Western deployments in the Arabian Sea.

The Kenyan Navy has a complex problem when it comes to choosing vessels. Though a large country, Kenya has only 500 miles of coast. Much of this is protected by huge fringeing reefs, an effective deterrent to illegal landings in even the most clement weather. The one main base, the fine harbour of Mombasa, is in the southern sector of the coast, so any worthwhile patrols off the border with Somalia would require a good range capability. At the same time, the

The Omani logistic landing ship *Al Munassir*. (*Mike Lennon*)

Top: British royal yacht *Britannia* proved remarkably effective in evacuating civilians of many nationalities during the coup fighting at Aden early in 1986. (*Royal Navy*)

Above: **Fast attack craft *Mamba* of the Kenyan Navy.**

conditions created by the north-east monsoon make intrusions very unlikely. The decision to build a force of 56m, 400-ton missile craft therefore seems logical, though it will not provide any means of surveillance in heavy weather, a task which will have to be performed by aircraft.

Kenya's southern neighbour, Tanzania, has few pretensions as a naval power and is too straitened to make plans in that direction. China's former influence lives on in the form of the Tanzam railway and the naval base at Dar-es-Salaam. The Chinese patrol craft transferred in the late 1960s and early 1970s are small and past their prime, but Beijing remains interested in its African toehold. This is also true of the Seychelles, whose other foreign contacts – principally the Soviet Union and Vietnam – probably prompted its support for the Soviet invasion of Afghanistan. The naval importance of the Seychelles and Tanzania lies entirely in their geographical situation and their possession of valuable harbours. Under present conditions neither is likely to welcome visits other than brief courtesy calls from Western navies. At the same time, the government of the Seychelles, in concert with Mauritius and Madagascar, has proclaimed a policy of non-alignment and rejection of foreign military and naval establishments.

The desperate and tragic condition of Mozambique makes any estimate of future trends there extremely difficult. China's interest in the country dates back to the support given to Frelimo when that organisation was operating from Tanzania before the Portuguese withdrawal in 1974. In 1977 a treaty of friendship was concluded with the Soviet Union, and the latter demonstrated her support for the government in Maputo in 1981 by deploying a small naval group to local ports in the wake of a South African raid on an ANC base in the capital. But South Africa plays an

South Africa's three *Daphne*-class patrol submarines – *Maria van Riebeeck, Emily Hobhouse* and *Johanna van der Merwe* – pictured off the strategically vital base of Simonstown. (*South African Navy*)

essential role in Mozambique's tattered economy, and Western aid has been sought to stave off disaster as the civil war absorbs more and more lives and money. The local naval force is of no significance, but the presence of Cuban troops and the series of safe havens available along the 1,200 miles of coastline are of major strategic importance. The current problems in South Africa mean that these factors could achieve even greater significance.

The main focus of armed opposition to the govern-

Eastern bloc, as evidenced by recent broadcasts from Addis Ababa. Were South African forces to move into Mozambique the USSR could well consider lending a hand under the 1977 treaty, if only through the use of surrogate troops. This may well be dismissed as fantasy but it is not unlike the scenarios which came to life in Afghanistan, Ethiopia and Vietnam. If it did materialise, the condition of the one state in Africa with a stable economy would be further eroded.

Whatever the political rights and wrongs of the situation in Southern Africa, certain naval facts are inescapable. For a start, the Republic of South Africa is a major trading partner of Britain, France, West Germany and the USA. Of the 20,000 or so merchant ships which double the Cape of Good Hope every year, at least a third call at the many efficient ports around the 1,000 miles of coastline between Cape Town and the north-eastern border. The naval base at Simonstown is the only fully effective centre for naval docking and repairs in the southern hemisphere between Australia and South America. Were there to be any interference with the Suez Canal-Red Sea route – the practicability of which was recently demonstrated by the Libyan minelaying expedition – the Cape route would be the only alternative. This would be impassable if a hostile-minded power assumed control in the Republic. Finally, Western manufacturers of both civil and military equipment rely heavily, and in some cases exclusively, on high-grade minerals from South Africa.

Foxtrot-class submarine *Karanj* of the Indian Navy. (*Giorgio Arra*)

The activities of the Soviets and their allies have not been to the liking of many African populations, and there is no evidence that the inhabitants of South Africa would like them any better. Any incursion in this region would certainly be gravely to the detriment of the West. But it is far harder to assess the impact of Soviet policies on Indian affairs. The government in Delhi is firmly committed to achieving dominance in the Indian Ocean area. While Nehru maintained a policy of worldwide interest, suitably distanced from the major power blocs, Indira Gandhi made "pre-eminence" the national goal. The war of 1971 carved off Bangladesh from Pakistan, and the process of achieving a greater India was under way. This short war focused attention in both India and Pakistan on the value of maritime power, and the Soviet Union, which had consistently endorsed Mrs Gandhi's view of the natural role of India, showed a willingness to provide naval aid.

Soviet squadrons had been deployed in the Indian Ocean since 1965, and in 1968 the first of eight Soviet Foxtrot-class submarines, accompanied by a depot ship, was transferred. The first major results of visits by high-placed Soviet officers in 1965, these vessels were followed in 1969 by the first of what became two squadrons of Petya-class frigates. Two years later eight Osa I missile craft were transferred in time to

ment in Pretoria is the African National Congress, whose guerillas operate from centres in the African states on South Africa's northern and eastern borders. "Hot pursuit" regularly results in South African troops crossing these borders and may sooner or later provoke an unexpected escalation. Despite Mozambique's agreement with South Africa to deny the ANC the shelter of her territory, this may be easier said than done. In addition to support from vocal Western groups, the ANC has the backing of the

Perfectly illustrating the shifting influences on the Indian Navy is the frigate *Talwar*, an ex-British *Whitby*-class ship retrofitted with Soviet SS-N-2 Styx anti-ship missiles.

carry out a bombardment of Karachi harbour during the 1971 war. Five years later eight Osa IIs were handed over, marking the beginning of a steady flow of ships and craft. Another five LSMs have followed the pair which arrived in 1966. This amphibious warfare squadron, now numbering seven Polnochny-class ships, is being steadily reinforced by indigenous building.

Complementing the landing ships and vital to the continued utility of harbours in wartime, six Natya-class ocean minesweepers arrived in 1978–80, to be followed by the same number of Yevgenya-class inshore minesweepers. The first of three Kashin II destroyers arrived in 1980 and a further three were ordered two years later. It is now reported that massive reinforcements in the form of six submarines (possibly of the modern Kilo class), two Kresta II cruisers, a further three Kashin II destroyers, up to five more missile corvettes, and six more locally built Polnochny-class LSMs are planned or building.

The Indian Navy also operates significant numbers of Western ships: an aircraft carrier, six *Leander*-class frigates built in Bombay plus three examples of a modified version, six elderly British frigates and a few auxiliaries. With yards in Bombay, Calcutta and Goa, further building to both Western and Soviet designs is probable, starting with the second pair of at least four, possibly six, West German Type 1500 submarines.

Thus by the early 1990s the strength of the Indian Navy could have reached 18 submarines, two aircraft carriers (with a third planned), two cruisers, nine destroyers (with a further group of Project 15 5,000-ton destroyers under construction), nine large frigates, ten small frigates, 14 missile corvettes, 14 missile craft, 13 LSMs, at least five major landing craft, 12

MSOs, six MSIs, six survey ships plus depot ships, tankers, repair ships, tugs and auxiliaries. Allowance has been made here for deletions but not for future orders. In addition, a well organised coastguard numbers five frigate-sized ships and two dozen various patrol craft.

The Indian Navy is divided into two fleets with three major shore commands. Flag officers also command in the Andaman Islands and at Goa. Main bases are at Bombay (Western Command) and Vishakapatnam (Eastern Command and submarine HQ). Cochin (Southern Command) has a naval air base, with others at Dabolim and Arakkonan; these are the shore stations for 20 elderly Seahawk fighters, 17 Alizé anti-submarine aircraft, eight maritime patrol aircraft, 32 helicopters and up to 40 training and utility aircraft.

The fact that a flag officer runs Goa tends to confirm reports of plans for a major naval base beyond the range of Pakistani strike aircraft. The commander in the Andamans also has a growing infrastructure, and it was there that the most recent large-scale amphibious exercise took place. There are unconfirmed reports of plans to set up facilities in the Nicobar Islands, south of the Andamans and straddling the entrance to the Malacca Strait.

The countries surrounding the Indian Ocean are beset by maritime problems, and any forecast of future trends must take account of a wealth of variables. Many of these are external. How will the situation in Israel affect the Gulf states and their Palestinian populations? Will the USSR find Afghanistan too indigestible a morsel? Will the first Chinese naval visit to the ocean be followed by a serious effort to achieve a position of influence? What will be the outcome of the crisis in South Africa? These are just a few of the imponderables which affect the future of this huge ocean area.

One thing seems to be constant, however, and that is the approach of India. Despite the successes of the moderate Rajiv Gandhi in a number of spheres, while the long-standing major policymakers of this huge land remain in positions of authority, the influence of one man may be insufficient to counter the current expansionist mood. And if India, with her overwhelming naval power, were to seek a position of pre-eminence not only in the sub-continent but also in the surrounding ocean and land areas, the major powers would be forced to react. Soviet plans would be in peril, American interests would be at risk, Chinese hopes of an Asian balance would be frustrated and the vital trade links of Europe and Japan would be threatened. The further arming of the Indian forces would do little to help the cause of world peace and could even provoke future hostilities.

Indian Navy ships like the Kashin II-class destroyer *Rana* are maintaining an ever higher profile in the region. Do India's expansionist ambitions augur well for peace? (*Selcuk Emre*)

Torpedoes for tomorrow

Cdr Roy Corlett RN

Roy Corlett joined the Royal Navy as an artificer in 1937 and subsequently served in submarines in all rates and ranks up to commander. His final RN appointment was as Staff Weapons Officer to Flag Officer Submarines. Following retirement he worked for Vickers Shipbuilding Ltd before setting up as a consultant to companies such as the torpedo manufacturers Gould of the USA and Whitehead of Italy.

The six Soviet Alfa-class submarines now at sea represent the beginning of a new era in underwater technology. With a speed in excess of 42kt and a maximum diving depth in the order of 3,000ft, they are some 40% faster than RN and USN fleet submarines and can dive to nearly twice the operating depth. Their hulls are made of titanium alloy, a material which American experts did not expect to see on a production line much before the 21st century. It seems likely that careful hull design, compliant coatings and other techniques to reduce drag and control the boundary layer are used to increase underwater speed. And there are good grounds for assuming that significant advances in power generation and propulsion technology have been developed and evaluated in the Victor III class and are now being incorporated into the latest Akula, Mike and Sierra-class fleet submarines. It is reasonable to forecast that before the end of the 1990s Soviet submarines will be able to exceed 50kt and dive to depths greater than 5,000ft. If war did break out, how and with what could the West attack and destroy them?

A nuclear depth charge has an estimated lethal radius of three miles and would be an effective area weapon against all classes of submarine. Such weapons used to be regarded as politically safe because at sea their effects could be closely confined to military targets. Fortunately, this dangerous philosophy appears to have been replaced by more realistic assessments of the probable repercussions, especially in a limited conflict like the Falklands War.

Ordinary depth charges or ASW missile-launching systems like the Bofors 375 are excellent deterrent devices and can provide a close-range defence against torpedo attack, but would take too long to sink to great depths.

Soviet Sierra-class attack submarine: setting the standard for Western torpedo designers.

Lightweight anti-submarine torpedoes can be delivered in a variety of ways. Possibly the speediest is by missile, as demonstrated here by the Australian/British Ikara. (*BAe*)

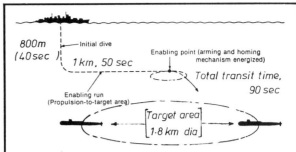

Fig 1 Performance of Stingray against the Soviet Alfa-class attack submarine. In the time it takes the torpedo to dive to operating depth, transit to the last known position of the submarine and arm itself, the target area will have expanded to a circle 1.8km in diameter

Stingray lightweight torpedo enters the water after an air drop. (*Marconi*)

The only option left is therefore the torpedo, of which there are two types. The lightweight ASW torpedo can be launched from surface ships and aircraft or transported to the launch area by airflight missile. The heavyweight dual-purpose torpedo can be fired from surface ships or submarines and is capable of attacking surface or submerged targets. Regardless of type, torpedo effectiveness can be summarised under three headings:

● **Performance** Enough speed to intercept and, if necessary, overtake a target and the endurance to run out to long ranges. To be effective a torpedo needs to be at least 50% faster than the target.

● **Attack capability** The ability either to home in on the target and strike it by means of an inbuilt active/passive sonar detection system, or to be guided by the firing ship or submarine. Modern torpedoes usually have both, plus the ability to counter evasive action by the target.

● **Lethality** Sufficient explosive power, either on striking the target or by detonating nearby, to destroy hull watertight integrity and cause the vessel to sink.

In assessing what the West may already have as a means of attacking high-speed submarines operating at great depths, the lightweight ASW torpedo can immediately be discounted. Figure 1 illustrates the worst case for this kind of weapon: a surface-launched Mk 46 or Stingray attacking an Alfa-class submarine proceeding at 42kt at 3,000ft. Both weapons have similar performance, in the order of 45kt maximum speed and 10km range. In more than two minutes' dead time between launch and the torpedo's arrival in the search area, the submarine could have moved to anywhere within a radius of nearly 1km. With less than 8km of range remaining and a speed advantage over the target of less than 3kt, the torpedo is highly unlikely to make a successful interception. Launch from an aircraft or a guided missile such as Ikara eliminates the 800m/40sec swim-out dead time of surface launch. But the time to reach a search depth of

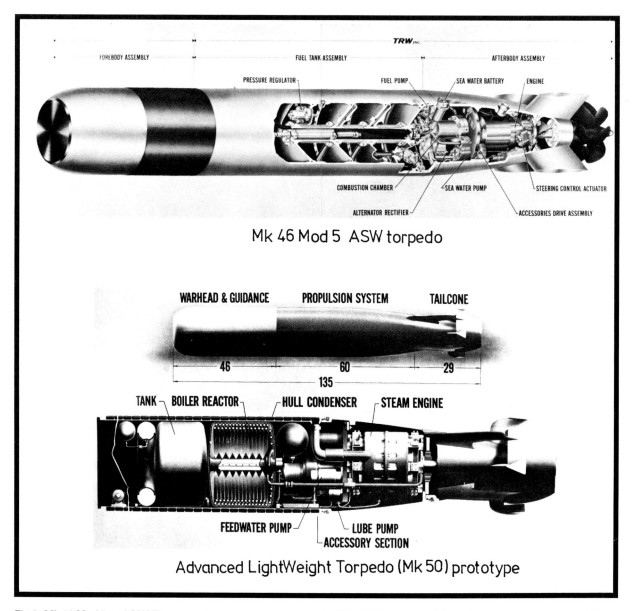

Mk 46 Mod 5 ASW torpedo

Advanced LightWeight Torpedo (Mk 50) prototype

Fig 2 Mk 46 Mod 5 and ALWT compared.

3,000ft remains the same at over 1min 20sec and target overtake speed is still limited to 3kt. Against an Alfa attack capability would be marginal if, as has been predicted, target maximum speed and depth increase to 50kt/1.5km (5,000ft) in the next ten years, while at maximum operating depth the target would always be able to outrun the weapon.

The American replacement for the Mk 46 Mod 5 torpedo is to be the Mk 50, formerly known as the Advanced Light Weight Torpedo (ALWT), a prototype of which is illustrated in Figure 2. Compared with the Mk 46, the Mk 50 is 15in longer and 50% heavier and delivers a 67kg warhead, 22kg more than the earlier weapon. Predicted performance

is 55kt/15km, a significant improvement on the Mk 46 and Stingray. But would this be enough to permit attacks on submarines faster and deeper diving than the Alfa? It seems unlikely.

Finally there is the question of lethality. Lightweight torpedoes explode on contact with the target. More modern weapons such as the Mk 50 and Stingray embody techniques which focus the explosive effect to optimise damage. Even so, the separation between the two hulls of the later classes of Soviet submarine should be sufficient to contain major damage and prevent penetration of the pressure hull.

Accounts of torpedo developments currently emphasise the importance of homing systems being "smart", or able to differentiate between target returns and the clutter of false signals from the surface, seabed or acoustic countermeasures launched by the target. Modern microprocessors and sophisticated

Test launch of an Advanced Light Weight Torpedo.
(*McDonnell Douglas*)

---

software mean that this is not too difficult to accomplish. The Post Detector Processor, to be fitted in the Mk 50 torpedo, and its operating principles are shown in Figure 3. But in the quest for smartness other, even more important, operational factors have been neglected. Homing intelligence is useless unless it is complemented by a propulsion system with the power to reach the target and a warhead with the potential energy to destroy it on arrival.

Of these requirements, the more urgent is a new torpedo propulsion system. A heavyweight dual-purpose torpedo is 533mm in diameter and about 6m long and weighs approximately 1.5 tonnes. The payload is a 250kg high-explosive warhead which can be detonated by either contact or proximity fuze. Nuclear warheads can also be fitted. Figure 4 shows three generations of heavyweight torpedo in outline. The G7A was the standard U-boat weapon during the Second World War. The SST/SUT was its post-war replacement and represents the technology of the early 1960s. The American Mk 48 ADCAP weapon is, as will be seen later, the only Western torpedo capable of being developed into a genuine threat to present and future Soviet nuclear submarines. These three weapons have a common problem: the excessive amount of volume taken up by their propulsive energy storage. Figure 5 shows how the performance of heavyweight and lightweight torpedoes is affected by extra power, and reveals that the 180kW and 55kt of the ALWT represent the best currently attainable by a light-weight. Existing technology might be stretched to

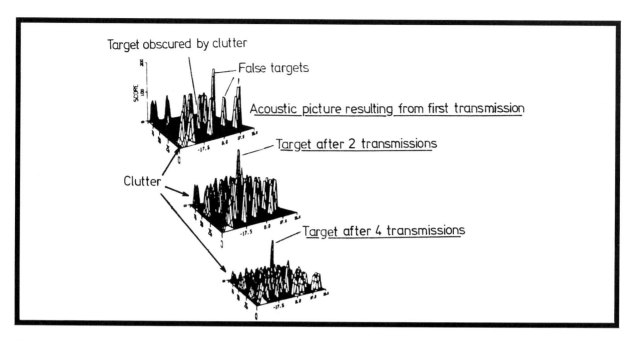

Fig 3 The Post Detection Processor fitted to ALWT analyses sonar returns repeatedly, discarding mid-water and bottom clutter and false returns to reveal the true position of the target.

Fig 4 Energy storage requirements of three generations of torpedo compared. Though the Mk 48 ADCAP represents a significant improvement on the two earlier designs, the proportion of its volume given over to fuel is still excessive.

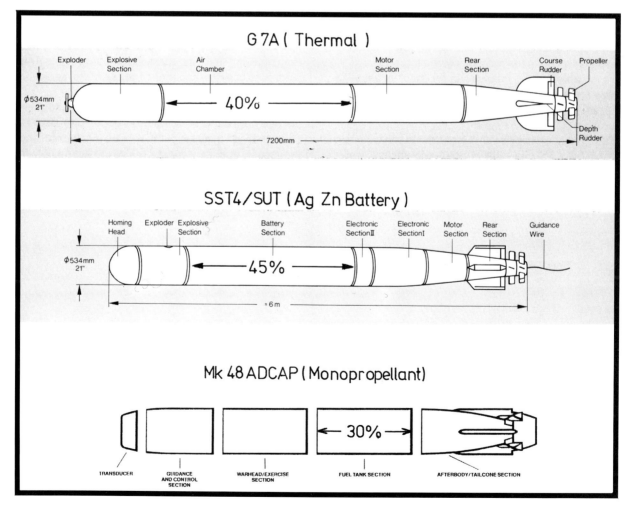

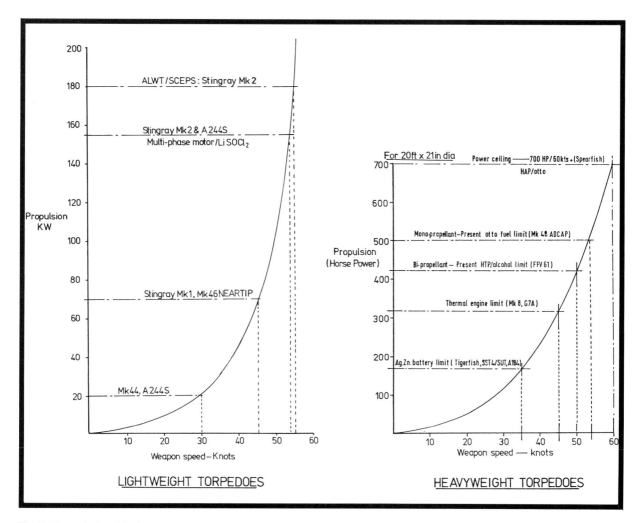

Fig 5 The relationship between power and speed in lightweight and heavyweight torpedoes. Comparison of the two curves suggests that there is little to be gained from increasing the power output of the present generation of lightweights.

---

yield 60kt and 20km range, but no more. Among the heavyweights the situation is more promising, as will be explained.

The G7A was a shallow-draught weapon, without guidance or homing systems; it has long been obsolete. The second generation of silver zinc battery-driven weapons – Tigerfish, SST/SUT, A 184 – have a maximum running speed of 35kt, a range of about 15km and a maximum running depth of about 380m. Their technology has reached a plateau which offers very little in the way of further development, and as instruments for attacking deep-diving Soviet submarines, they are also obsolete.

The Mk 48 ADCAP is the present last word in a long line of development. Exact performance is not known but is probably in the region of 60kt/30km. It is known that it can operate at depths exceeding 900m

(over 3,000ft). Further increases in performance will however require the development of a new propulsion system, one capable of coping with the penalties imposed by the phenomenon of backpressure.

Atmospheric pressure at sea level is about 15lb/in². Due to the weight of water, this increases by a factor of 0.444 for each extra foot of depth. Thus at a depth of 3,000ft the pressure is $15+(3,000\times0.444)=$ 1,347lb/in²; at 5,000ft it is 2,235lb/in². All existing thermal propulsion systems exhaust into the water and so are subject to a backpressure which increases with running depth. This is an operational disadvantage for an external combustion piston engine like that fitted to the Mk 48 ADCAP, though the operating cycle can contain the problem. Assume for example that a Mk 48 engine combustion chamber pressure of 7,000lb/in² yields 500hp against a backpressure of 28lb/in² at a running depth of 30ft. At 3,000ft, with the combustion chamber pressure increased by the equivalent of the backpressure – 7,000 + 1,347 = 8,347lb/in² – the power output will remain the same. The penalty is increased fuel consumption.

With a turbine like the 21TP04 developed by Sundstrand for the British Spearfish torpedo,

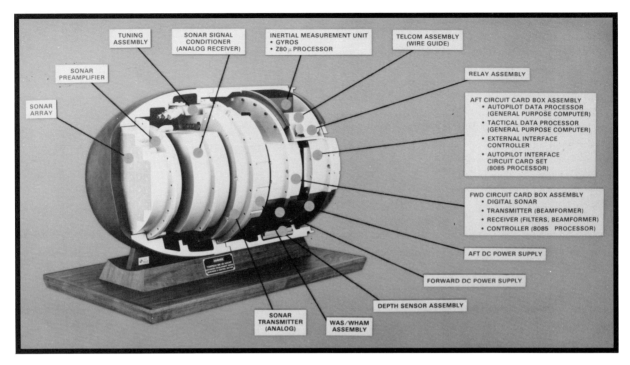

Homing head of the Mk 48 ADCAP. (*Hughes*)

increased operating depth raises more complex problems. Unlike a piston engine, a turbine is not driven by linear expansion, but by the kinetic energy of gas jets impinging upon the turbine blades and rotating them. The criterion for operating efficiency is the ratio between the gas pressures at inlet and exhaust. At a running depth of 30ft, assuming the same combustion chamber pressure as in the Mk 48 torpedo, the ratio is $7,000lb/in^2$ (combustion chamber): $28lb/in^2$ (backpressure)$=250:1$. However, at a running depth of 3,000ft the ratio drops to $7,000lb/in^2$: $1,347lb/in^2 = 5:1$. To achieve any useful work at all the maximum pressure ratio should be at least 50:1, which would require a combustion chamber pressure of $1,347lb/in^2$ (backpressure)$\times 50 = 67,350lb/in^2$.

Even if a radical increase in fuel consumption were acceptable, it is extremely unlikely that a combustion chamber capable of withstanding such tremendous pressures or a fuel pump able to inject monopropellant against such a head could be designed. Further, even

Spearfish, Britain's latest heavyweight torpedo. (*Marconi*)

if such a pump proved feasible, the take-off of power from the turbine to drive it would be excessive. Some improvement might result from the use of a more energetic fuel, but otherwise all the evidence suggests that turbines cannot be made to work effectively against the backpressures which would be encountered when attacking submarines at great depths. Further increases in running depth may be feasible with the piston engine, but the increase in fuel consumption would result in an unacceptable reduction in range. Thus if the Alfa-class is to be countered, and if it is accepted that even faster/deeper diving Soviet submarines may already be at sea, the open-cycle turbine propulsion of Spearfish is already obsolete and the Mk 48 ADCAP's capability cannot be stretched much further. What is needed by both weapons is a high-energy propulsion system which is unaffected by running depth.

Figure 6 shows how rapidly open-exhaust systems waste energy in overcoming backpressure. Although there is a crossover point above which the open cycle is more efficient, the steady power output of a closed cycle has very significant advantages when running deep. Closed-cycle propulsion is unaffected by backpressure because there is no exhaust. A typical example of present technology is the battery and

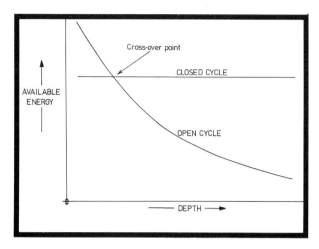

Fig 6 The effect of the increase in backpressure with depth on the power output of an open-cycle propulsion system.

electric motor, as fitted in Tigerfish, SST/SUT and A 184 torpedoes. But the power which can be delivered is totally inadequate, even for present requirements. By far the most promising alternative is the closed-cycle thermal system known as SCEPS (Stored Chemical Energy Propulsion System), shown in Figure 7.

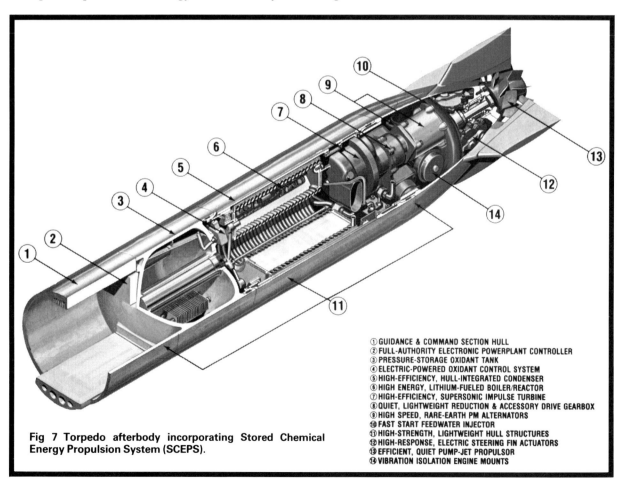

Fig 7 Torpedo afterbody incorporating Stored Chemical Energy Propulsion System (SCEPS).

① GUIDANCE & COMMAND SECTION HULL
② FULL-AUTHORITY ELECTRONIC POWERPLANT CONTROLLER
③ PRESSURE-STORAGE OXIDANT TANK
④ ELECTRIC-POWERED OXIDANT CONTROL SYSTEM
⑤ HIGH-EFFICIENCY, HULL-INTEGRATED CONDENSER
⑥ HIGH ENERGY, LITHIUM-FUELED BOILER/REACTOR
⑦ HIGH-EFFICIENCY, SUPERSONIC IMPULSE TURBINE
⑧ QUIET, LIGHTWEIGHT REDUCTION & ACCESSORY DRIVE GEARBOX
⑨ HIGH SPEED, RARE-EARTH PM ALTERNATORS
⑩ FAST START FEEDWATER INJECTOR
⑪ HIGH-STRENGTH, LIGHTWEIGHT HULL STRUCTURES
⑫ HIGH-RESPONSE, ELECTRIC STEERING FIN ACTUATORS
⑬ EFFICIENT, QUIET PUMP-JET PROPULSOR
⑭ VIBRATION ISOLATION ENGINE MOUNTS

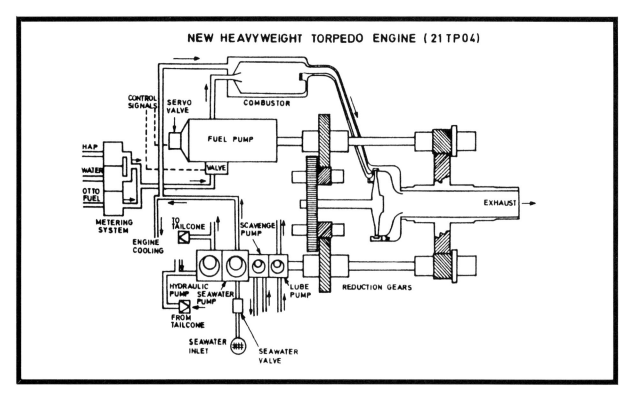

NEW HEAVYWEIGHT TORPEDO ENGINE (21TP04)

Fig 8 Layout of the Sundstrand HAP/Otto engine developed to power the British Spearfish heavyweight torpedo. (*Sundstrand Aerospace*)

The chemical in SCEPS is sulphur hexafluoride, a non-toxic and stable gas which is five times heavier than air. The fuel is lithium. Heat is generated when the two are brought into contact. The heat is used to boil water into steam, which drives a turbine and is then condensed in a heat-exchanger and returned to the boiler. The cycle is simple to explain but some very sophisticated engineering has been needed to produce reliable hardware. Because it is a single-stage unit, the turbine must run at high speed – typically about 150,000rpm – to extract useful energy from the steam. Less than two litres of water circulate continuously in states varying from superheated steam to liquid. The technical difficulties have been great but it is believed that SCEPS, as fitted in the Honeywell Mk 50 torpedo, is now working reliably. It is currently proposed to scale up the system to create depth-independent closed-cycle propulsion for heavyweight torpedoes. Preliminary calculations suggest that this is feasible and that power outputs of at least 800hp could be expected.

If large quantities of energy are contained within a small volume, any accident usually results in an explosion. The difficulty lies in deciding how large a reduction in submarine safety can be accepted in return for the storage of large quantities of energy in a

torpedo. The most compact source of thermal energy is the monopropellant, a substance containing both fuel and the oxygen to combust it. "Monopropellant" is also a euphemism for an explosive substance. The best known torpedo monopropellant is a heavily modified form of nitroglycerine called Otto fuel, which propels the Mk 48 torpedo. So safe that it is classified as a low-risk fire hazard, Otto fuel is also comparatively low in energy yield, with only 50% of the potential capable of being extracted to perform useful work.

The Sundstrand turbine fitted in Spearfish increases energy yield from 50% to an estimated 87% by combining an extra oxidant, hydroxyl amine perchlorate (HAP), with Otto fuel. According to press reports, there have already been a number of explosions, which suggests that it is unwise to presume on Otto fuel's excellent safety record. And although some of the exhaust products of the new mixture are soluble in water, which will improve the turbine pressure ratio, the potential hazard to the carrier submarine far outweighs any propulsion improvements. The closed-cycle SCEPS therefore still seems the best development path for thermal systems.

It is likely that by the end of this decade a new generation of high-capacity batteries will have been developed to drive high-speed multi-phase motors through thyristor converters. Taking the magnesium/silver chloride seawater battery which powers Stingray as typifying current technology, the volumetric efficiency of aluminium/silver oxide represents a threefold energy increase, while lithium/thionyl

chloride has even greater power storage potential. However, there are at least two difficult design problems to be solved before these new energy sources can safely be tapped:
• High currents generate intense magnetic fields which interfere with the electronics and microcomputers of the sonar homing and weapon control systems.

Fig 9 This comparison of torpedo energy sources reveals that although every one apart from the magnesium/silver chloride battery still has plenty of development potential, the very high maximum values promised by aluminium/silver oxide and lithium/thionyl chloride batteries could well see these systems winning the day over even the most advanced thermal solutions.

Source	Energy Yield			
	kW min /litre		kw min /kg	
	Present	Future	Present	Future
Thermal				
Otto fuel (Mk 48 ADCAP)	18.9	22.8	18.6	22.4
SCEPS (Mk 50)	16.8	25.0	10.5	18.0
Primary Batteries				
Magnesium/Silver Chloride (Sting Ray)	9.6	9.6	5.9	5.9
Aluminium/Silver Oxide (Future	–	28.8	–	12.0
Lithium Thionyl Chloride Developments)	19.2	31.8	8.8	33.0

• Energy density can only be increased by packing in as many positive and negative electrodes as possible. This means reducing to the minimum the separation between them, which increases the risk of an electrical short-circuit and a violent explosion.

Figure 10 is an artist's impression of an advanced power unit for a lightweight torpedo. Transistor inverters convert the lithium/thionyl chloride battery's DC output to high-voltage AC to drive a multi-phase motor at high speed. This arrangement reduces power losses and also results in an extremely compact motor. Motor output is passed through a traction-roller speed-reducer before coupling with either contra-rotating propellers or a pump jet; the elimination of gear teeth greatly reduces radiated noise. In a simple and reliable arrangement, the inverter, motor and speed-reducer are cooled and lubricated by a common fluid plus heat-exchanger.

As well as closed-cycle operation, the powerplants of tomorrow's torpedoes will also need increased energy densities if the required higher speeds and longer ranges are to be attained. New types of battery driving high-speed AC motors have promise, though so far as

Fig 10 Lithium/thionyl chloride battery-based propulsion unit for a lightweight torpedo.

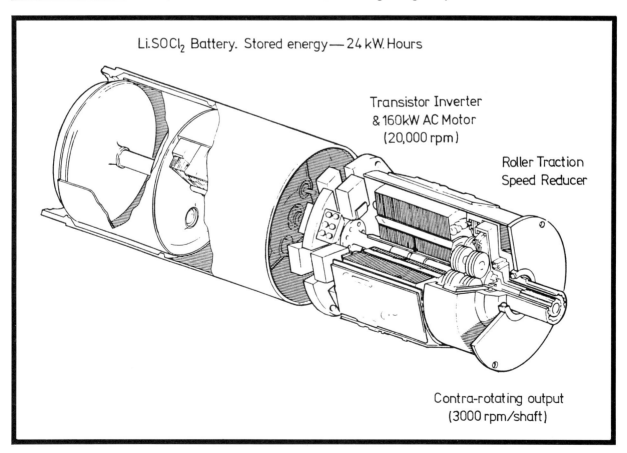

Li.SOCl₂ Battery. Stored energy — 24 kW. Hours

Transistor Inverter & 160kW AC Motor (20,000 rpm)

Roller Traction Speed Reducer

Contra-rotating output (3000 rpm/shaft)

heavyweight torpedoes are concerned such systems have yet to leave the drawing board.

The power increases needed over the next decade will have to be matched by more efficient ways of converting motor output into thrust. For many years the contra-rotating propeller has been the standard solution, and it is still the norm in nearly all contemporary heavyweight torpedoes. The exception is the Mk 48 ADCAP, which uses a pump jet. This is best described as an open single-stage turbine with the rotor revolving between two stators attached to the torpedo tailcone, the whole being enclosed by a close-fitting annular shroud. The main advantages of this system are:

● Propulsor efficiency increases with rotational speed of the rotor and weapon velocity. (Propeller efficiency decreases with speed.)

● Cavitation, which reduces coupling efficiency and generates noise, is easier to control.

With careful design of weapon shape, the pump jet can also reduce drag by containing the boundary layer.

Experimental work has been carried out with magnetohydrodynamic (MHD) devices. These systems convert electrical power into magnetic pulses which couple to the water to generate forward motion. Calculations suggest that this method would be extremely efficient, and circumstantial evidence indicates that it may already be at sea as a cruise propulsor in Victor III, Sierra and Akula-class submarines. There is a remote possibility that MHD may soon be applied to Soviet torpedoes, but it is unlikely to be a practical proposition before the next century. For one thing, the problems of scaling down the technology are enormous. Pump jet improvements are more likely in the next 10–15 years, possibly centring on the development of multiple stages to increase the volume within which torque can be converted to thrust and so improve control over the boundary layer and water turbulence.

Propulsion system advances are likely to be matched by developments aimed at reducing the resistance of the water to the torpedo's passage through it. The energy needed to propel a torpedo is expended in:

1 Forcing aside the molecules of water so that the weapon may pass.

2 Overcoming the friction of the water against the outer skin of the weapon. This and the next two forces are all forms of "drag".

3 Overcoming the retarding force created when the laminar flow of water past the weapon is converted into turbulence.

4 Overcoming the extra drag created at the rear end of the torpedo as the separated water flows rejoin.

Laminar flow is what should happen in the liquid surrounding the torpedo, with the water molecules

Fig 11 Pump-jet propulsion system of the US Mk 48 torpedo.

Fig 12 Optimum configuration for a torpedo afterbody incorporating a pump jet with boundary-layer intake. Compare this with the working design shown in Fig 11.

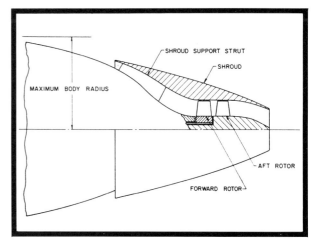

moving in well ordered sheets within the **boundary layer**, where this movement is taking place. Energy losses in this category are due mainly to surface roughness of the weapon. Any discontinuity, such as a recessed screw, is sufficient to disrupt laminar flow.

Turbulence is the breaking up of a smooth flow into random molecular motions which interact to increase drag significantly. In addition to surface discontinuities, protrusions such as topstops, side runners and tail fins all generate turbulence.

Finally, if the water molecules within the boundary layer can rejoin without major discontinuities after the passage of the torpedo, there will be minimum after drag. Ideally, the afterbody and propulsor(s) should be designed so that the boundary layer is contained within the shroud and passed through the pump jet. This helps to reduce drag and the wake turbulence behind the weapon. Figure 12 shows a torpedo afterbody shape and pump jet designed for boundary layer intake. It is interesting to compare this optimum shape with Figure 11, which shows how the design actually evolved with the Mk 48 torpedo.

The negative effects of drag and turbulence increase with speed. A well established formula for calculating the onset of turbulence due to surface roughness is:

$$\frac{6 \times 10^{-2}}{\text{weapon speed in knots}}$$

This reveals that a surface discontinuity of as little as 0.002in is enough to disturb laminar flow on a torpedo travelling at 60kt.

Having packed in the maximum amount of potential energy to drive a highly efficient closed-cycle power unit and pump jet, removed all unnecessary protrusions and polished the skin of the torpedo to a mirror finish, the last avenue for performance improvement is a change of shape. The effect that this would have is demonstrated in Figure 13.

Dolphin 1 was an optimum shape evaluated by North American, the aerospace corporation, in the early 1960s. It was a gravity-powered fin-stabilised body with a 3.33 length:diameter ratio and 5.6ft³ volume. Being negatively buoyant, it attained speeds in excess of 60kt when dropped vertically into the sea. Expendable ballast was shed at a controlled depth and Dolphin 1 returned to the surface, where data-recording equipment was removed and the records analysed. The following results were of particular interest:

1 Drag was 60% lower than with a conventional torpedo shape. This was attributed to improved laminar flow over the surface of the body.

2 When the boundary layer was deliberately disrupted, turbulence resulted and drag increased to the same figure as for a conventional torpedo shape.

The only real value of this experiment was to

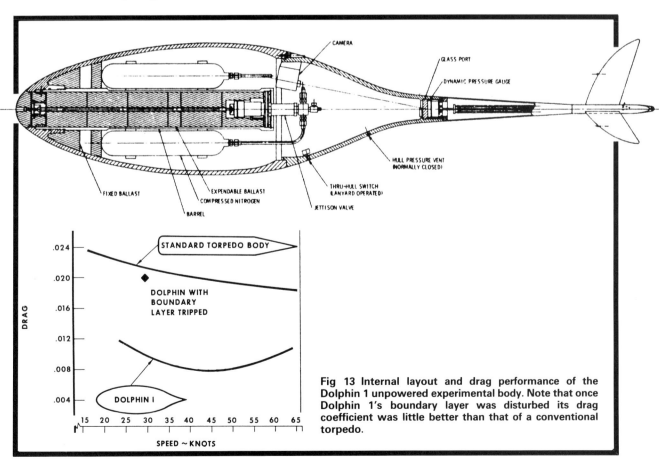

Fig 13 Internal layout and drag performance of the Dolphin 1 unpowered experimental body. Note that once Dolphin 1's boundary layer was disturbed its drag coefficient was little better than that of a conventional torpedo.

demonstrate the importance of preventing the onset of turbulence. But unfortunately a torpedo's shape and dimensions are controlled by the tube from which it is discharged. Torpedo tubes are designed to contain a weapon 21in in diameter and about 20ft long. Any deviation from these parameters would entail radical alterations to the shape of the submarine. At least, that is the way things are in the West. The Soviet Union does not seem to be so constrained.

According to a report in *The Sunday Times* on November 18, 1984, the Soviet Union has developed a new torpedo, the Type 65. It is 26in in diameter and 30ft long, and can travel 50km at 50kt or 100km at 30kt. The propulsion system is probably a multi-piston engine fuelled with alcohol and using as oxidant high-test hydrogen peroxide (HTP). Given an estimated energy yield of 34kW/min/litre and 35kW/min/kg, this system should develop nearly twice as much usable power as a similar engine running on Otto fuel. The exhaust is steam, which can be condensed in a closed cycle to make weapon performance independent of running depth.

The use of high-test peroxide as an oxidant and fuel additive is not new. The main technical problems to be overcome are its instability; affinity for all organic substances, which usually results in an explosion; and ability to corrode almost any material with the exception of ultra-pure aluminium and some modern plastics. Sweden has used an alcohol/peroxide fuel mix in heavyweight anti-ship torpedoes for many years and claims never to have had a resulting serious accident. The American Mk 16 used a similar mix, which was finally withdrawn from service in 1975. It is known that Navol, the US Navy's version of high-test peroxide, caused a number of exciting incidents during its 20 years in service. British experiments with HTP ceased abruptly in 1955, when a trial torpedo exploded and sank HMS *Sidon*. However, the Russians must have full confidence in their new weapon and the submarine safety of its propulsion system, since a retrofit programme appears to be in hand, with four of the six bow torpedo tubes being removed from later classes of Soviet submarine and replaced with launching arrangements compatible with the new weapon.

But why the significant increase in size? The answer possibly lies in the contention that energy storage space – and hence performance – increases as a function of weapon size. A bigger torpedo can also carry more payload, and present estimates suggest that the warhead contains not less than 400kg of high explosive.

It is not possible to analyse all the factors likely to affect the development of future underwater weapons in an article of this length. We have concentrated here on the need to improve performance by increasing energy storage and power output and making the latter independent of running depth for one major reason: however intelligent a weapon may be in detecting and tracking, it will fail if it lacks the performance to overtake and hit the target, or to operate at the latter's maximum diving depth. There is, however, another reason for looking closely at propulsion, and that is the growing difference in the thinking behind Western and Soviet submarine operations. SSN-21, first of the class that will succeed the *Los Angeles*-class fleet submarine, will be designed for a top speed of only 35kt and, by inference, a maximum diving depth inferior to that of the Soviet Alfa. Because the Mk 48 torpedo can operate at the maximum diving depth of the Alfa, this is deemed to be sufficient. The main thrust of the SSN-21 design will be increased quietness, which is considered vital. Thus attack capability will be concentrated in the weapon rather than the launching platform, the ability of which to lie silently in wait to ambush the enemy being regarded as far more important than parity of speed and diving depth.

The Mk 48 torpedo is a fine, reliable weapon, proven by thousands of in-water trials and constantly improved over the years in response to sea experience and by the incorporation of new technology. The latest development, the ADCAP, is probably capable of attacking and destroying an Alfa operating at top speed and maximum diving depth. But the performance of its open-cycle piston engine propulsion system can be stretched no further; the fuel-consumption penalty is too high. In this respect it is today's torpedo, not a weapon for tomorrow. To keep abreast of Soviet submarine development, closed-cycle propulsion should have replaced the present open-exhaust system before the middle of the 1990s. A development of SCEPS would appear to be the only way of holding the fort until the high-energy batteries and motors under development become available early in the next century.

The introduction of six completely new classes of submarine between 1980 and 1983 indicates a continuing Soviet interest in the evolution of underwater technology. Novel shapes are emerging and great attention is being paid to compliant coatings and other methods of drag reduction, boundary-layer control and the elimination of turbulence. All the signs are that in the years ahead Soviet submarines will travel faster and dive deeper. The designers of tomorrow's torpedoes must take account of this primary challenge, starting with the development of propulsion systems which will allow the new weapons to travel at least 50% faster and outdive the enemy. If Western navies are to get ahead of the game once more, torpedo designers should be aiming now for 80kt, a maximum operating depth of 2,000m and a top-speed range of not less than 30nm.

Ruling the airwaves: electronic warfare at sea

Martin Streetly

Atlantic Conveyor, a victim of the vagaries of electronic warfare at sea. This British container ship, laden with helicopters and other military supplies during the Falklands War, burned out and sank after being struck by an Exocet anti-ship missile believed to have been decoyed away from the carrier *Invincible*.

Naval use of electronic warfare (EW) – the disruption of the enemy's communications and radar systems by electronic means, together with the exploitation of his electromagnetic emissions for tactical or strategic advantage – has a history stretching back to the earliest years of this century. Since 1939 the ever-increasing reliance on electronics, especially radar, in naval warfare has stimulated the evolution of seaborne countermeasures. Most recently, the threat posed by the radar-guided anti-shipping missile (ASM) has pushed naval electronic warfare to the point where it is now no exaggeration to claim that a warship's EW fit is as important to its survival and operational effectiveness as any other system. Nevertheless, EW remains perhaps the least understood of the military technologies.

It fell to the Royal Navy to introduce EW to the naval arena. As early as 1902 British radio operators were disrupting the opposition's radio communications during fleet exercises by means of jamming, and the concept spread through the world's navies thereafter. Two years later, during the Russo-Japanese War of 1904, communications jamming was used operationally for the first time in a naval engagement when Japanese fall-of-shot transmissions were disrupted during the bombardment of Port Arthur.

By the outbreak of the First World War the concept of EW had been firmly established in naval doctrine, and the Royal Navy was quick to use its expertise against the German Fleet. Indeed, the first recorded instance of such activity took place on the day *before* the official start of hostilities when, on August 4, 1914, the British cruisers *Indomitable* and *Indefatigable* "attempted to systematically jam" the wireless communications of the German warships *Goeben* and *Breslau*. Not content with such active measures, the Admiralty took the radio war much further, capitalising on its potential as an intelligence and location tool. German naval radio transmissions were monitored throughout the war and became the primary source of intelligence on the enemy's intentions. From 1915 onwards a chain of radio direction-finding stations was established along the British east coast to plot hostile activity on and above the North Sea.

By 1918 much of the philosophy of naval EW had been solidly established. Warships had used offensive jamming regularly, and the intelligence value of radio intercepts was well understood. But the cast of mind needed to derive the maximum benefit from the new technology had proved less easily developed. During the Battle of Jutland in 1916, for example, although Admiral Jellicoe was thoroughly familiar with the value of radio intelligence he had failed to ask the right questions of the available data. It seems not to have occurred to the Royal Navy's commanders that the enemy might suspect that their radio net was being tapped and act accordingly. This was indeed the case and the Germans had in fact instituted a campaign of deception to fool eavesdroppers. Thus on the eve of the battle, Jellicoe asked his intelligence service "Where is the callsign of the German flagship?" instead of explicitly calling for the enemy commander's location. He thus betrayed an ignorance of the cardinal rule of EW: that it is a double-edged weapon which can be quickly turned to an enemy's advantage by deception. The Royal Navy's intelligence service was well aware of the German practice of using false callsigns to deceive. But Jellicoe apparently was not and, crucially, he was not told of his mistake. This was not to be the last time that junior officers would fail to correct their commander's misapprehension of a new technology.

The Second World War further broadened the scope of naval EW, stimulating the increased use of electronics, especially radar, and the development of the air-launched ASM. The introduction of radar for gunlaying and sea and air search, and as an increasingly important adjunct to carrierborne air power had a profound effect on EW development at sea. While the vulnerability of radio communications was correctly appreciated (except, curiously, by the German Navy's submarine arm) and protective measures introduced, the strengths and weaknesses of radar were less clearly understood at first. The Royal Navy's response was to counsel radar silence, as in the case of HMS *Hood* during the last stages of the action against the *Bismarck* in 1941. It was also believed that radar signals, with their short pulse duration, would be harder to intercept than radio transmissions. But such difficulties as existed were soon overcome and by mid-war seaborne radar intercept receivers were regularly to be found alongside the more familiar radio interception and direction-finding equipment in many classes of Allied warship.

Radar jamming appeared rather later, being used principally in the great air-sea battles in the Pacific during 1944–45. True enough, the Germans had jammed British coastal radars during the "Channel Dash" of 1941 but the technique seems not to have been commonly used during ship-to-ship combat in the European and Atlantic theatres. There were however significant applications of radar jamming in two other areas. Extensive deception jamming from

Radars are the prime targets for offensive electronic warfare measures. This is the Marconi 805SW lightweight dual-radar tracker, associated with the British Seawolf point-defence system. (*Marconi*)

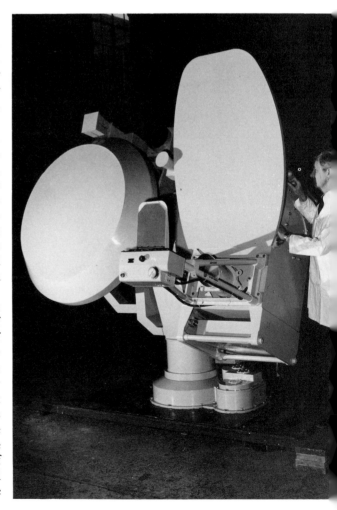

seaborne platforms was directed against the German coastal radar net during the D-Day landings, and a big effort went into countering the radio control systems of the Luftwaffe's Hs293 and Fritz-X air-launched anti-shipping weapons. The Hs293 glider bomb made its appearance during August 1943, when it was used to sink a corvette and damage another in the Bay of Biscay. Following the Italian capitulation, the even more lethal Fritz-X "smart" bomb accounted for the battleship *Roma*. Both weapons could be launched from beyond the range of the shipboard anti-aircraft defences at the time, and were only really vulnerable to electronic interference of their control systems.

In response to this threat two US Navy destroyers were equipped with suitable search receivers and jamming units and sent in October 1943 to the Mediterranean, where the new weapons were being most commonly used. The EW equipment proved effective after some modification and was used as a model for production units, which were first used in support of the Anzio landings in January 1944. Thereafter all convoys operating in the area included at least two ships equipped with jammers, and no further vessels were lost to missile attack. Similar equipment was used in support of the landings in Normandy and the South of France, and succeeded in defeating Fritz-X and Hs293 attacks against both invasion fleets.

By late 1944 the US Navy was working towards a standard EW fit, with surface ships from destroyers upwards receiving a radio direction-finder, an intercept receiver, a radar direction-finder, and a jamming capability which was usually directed at radar frequencies. At the same time the USN developed an extensive operational philosophy. Thus by the end of the war a US Navy task force operating

Some things have remained unchanged despite four decades of intensive electronic warfare development. HMS *Sheffield* was knocked out while acting as a radar picket in the same way as the anti-aircraft early-warning destroyers disposed around US task forces in the Pacific in 1945. (*John G. Callis*)

in the Pacific would be supported by radar picket ships stationed 20 to 40 miles out from the main force to give early warning of air attack; screening destroyers disposed "in such a manner that they could search for enemy radar signals, barrage and spot jam when ordered, or deceive the enemy by means of . . . shell Window"; and basic jamming equipment spread throughout the remainder of the force "to create maximum confusion to the enemy's radar presentation and lend additional protection to the interior units if the enemy should penetrate the screen." Supplement the picket ship with an airborne radar platform, add an airborne jamming capability and generally update the electronics, and you have the EW disposition of the USN's current battle groups.

The description of the screening destroyer's role mentions "barrage" and "spot" jamming and the deception measure known as "shell Window". These are typical of the language which continues to mystify even military professionals. Any understanding of EW must begin with its vocabulary. The most fundamental electronic warfare measure is jamming, or the disruption of radio and radar systems through the introduction of unwanted signals. Jamming can be active or passive. Active measures transmit a disruptive signal, while passive types reflect a radar's own emissions back at it to produce a spurious picture.

Active jammers can be divided into "brute force" and "deception" systems. The former can be used against both radio and radar and operate by saturating the target's receiver with electronic noise to blot out the desired signal. The most common variants of this type of jammer are the "spot" and "barrage" units, directed at a specific frequency or a range of frequencies respectively. Brute-force jammers predominated up to the end of the Second World War and for some time afterwards. More recently they have been joined by the much more subtle deception systems.

The deception jammer works by re-radiating or simulating a signal identical with the one generated by the target radar. This fake transmission is then fed back in such a way as to produce a genuine-looking but inaccurate presentation on the operator's screen. The beauty of this type of countermeasure is that its output does not look like jamming – unlike the brute-force methods, which are instantly recognisable for what they are. Against this, deception equipment is more complex and therefore more expensive, and also requires more intelligence groundwork to determine the target system's characteristics, which must be accurately reproduced if the simulation is to be convincing.

A French Dagaie chaff rocket launcher fires a salvo . . .

. . . and a decoy cloud blooms behind the frigate *Commandant Bory*. (*CSEE*)

A chaff rocket is loaded into a Plessey Shield decoy launcher. (*Plessey*)

Passive measures are in some ways similar but work by simply reflecting the target system's own signal and swamping it with return echoes. Forms of passive countermeasure include airborne reflectors towed aloft by ships or suspended from or hung inside balloons and, perhaps the most important, chaff. Known as Window during the Second World War, chaff takes the form of aluminium-foil strips carefully sized to a proportion of the target system's wavelength. When released in large quantities into the radar's transmission beam the strips generate a cloud of target echoes which masks the real threat. The cloud can also appear to a missile guidance radar as a target which is clearer and therefore more attractive than the real thing. Chaff can be loaded into shells and fired from a conventional deck gun, or dispensed by specialised launchers. It has become increasingly important as a seaborne EW measure, and now most front-line warships carry chaff systems for self-protection.

The end of hostilities in 1945 saw most of the building blocks of current naval EW – jammers, passive measures, direction-finders and intercept receivers – in place. Much of the operational doctrine

had also been laid down. By the last two years of the war air attack had become the most pressing threat and seaborne EW measures had been largely tailored to this new challenge. The importance of signals interception as a means of detecting an attack without revealing one's own position had been realised. This last capability has since assumed crucial importance in the latest round of the game, combating today's air-to-surface missiles.

The first clear indication of the power of these weapons came in October 1967 when the Israeli destroyer *Eilat* was sunk by three Styx ASMs fired from Egyptian Komar-class missile boats. The Soviet-manufactured Styx, which entered service in 1959–60, was the first modern ASM to be used operationally. Relatively large and slow by today's standards, Styx nevertheless presented the West with something of a headache. While its combined autopilot/radio command and active radar guidance system could be countered electronically, the rapid advances of the time raised the spectre of a homing system which could actually use the jamming signals intended to defeat it as a guidance medium. But despite the relative crudity of such first-generation ASMs, their speed and size made them very difficult targets for contemporary anti-aircraft weapons, leaving electronic countermeasures as the only practicable defence.

Most important of these techniques was the use of signals interception, now known as electronic support measures (ESM), to give early warning of the approach of the active guidance systems typical of ASMs. This was combined with close control of transmissions to prevent the use of homing heads, and passive measures, primarily chaff, to decoy the missile away from the target. Most recently, last-ditch ultra-rapid-firing guns have been added to this array in the hope of blowing the missile apart with an almost solid wall of shot if all else fails.

In spite of the high degree of automation now possible, the effectiveness of such measures remains a matter of human judgement, as the Falklands War showed in 1982. In that conflict, the Argentinian Air Force succeeded in knocking out the Type 42 destroyer *Sheffield* – well equipped with ESM and chaff launchers – and sinking the merchantman *Atlantic Conveyor* with Exocet ASMs. It now seems likely that *Sheffield*'s ESM suite was not operating because it would have interfered with her satellite communications system, which was in use at the crucial time. The problem of mutual interference amongst the various electronic systems carried by modern warships is growing in difficulty, and often fails to reveal itself until all the systems are operated in concert and under operational conditions.

Paradoxically, the loss of the *Atlantic Conveyor* has been attributed to the *successful* use of anti-ASM EW. At the time of the attack the Argentinian pilots were

Komar-class missile craft launches a Styx anti-ship missile. It was the loss of the Israeli destroyer *Eilat* in a Styx attack that awakened the world's navies to their vulnerability to the ASM. (*Tass*)

searching for the carrier *Invincible*. It is suggested that, having been detected, *Invincible* decoyed the Exocet away, only to see it then make for the very attractive radar target represented by the *Atlantic Conveyor*. Though this account has not been confirmed, it does however illustrate very well some of the hazards of EW operations in modern combat.

In spite of these problems the world's navies have come to terms with the possibility of attack by a single radar-guided ASM. But in the meantime the game has moved on, and now the threat has become a salvo of such weapons, fired from different directions and platforms and probably using a variety of guidance

Right: **Last line of defence against the anti-ship missile: Phalanx radar-directed gun system aboard HMS *Invincible*.** (*L. & L. van Ginderen*)

techniques. Even if such an attack were made up entirely of radar-guided weapons, the sheer weight of incoming signals and the speed of the attacking missiles would make computer control of the defences imperative. Decisions on the nature of the threat, the priority to be given to its various components, and the required response would have to be made in microseconds. While such systems have in fact entered service, they depend on complex software which is liable to programming bugs that can only be detected when the equipment is put to use. A good example of this phenomenon is the American AEGIS computer-controlled naval surface-to-air missile system, which was designed to handle up to 16 different targets simultaneously. Today, almost two decades after its inception, AEGIS has only ever managed four simultaneous engagements and is still having its software debugged.

Intense signal traffic is not the only new problem faced by the EW designer. The variety of emissions has also increased enormously. Amongst radars alone, modern ESM systems are faced with traditional pulsed emissions, continuous-wave transmissions and, most recently, "exotic" systems. The last are, for example, "frequency-agile", or capable of shifting

Exocet anti-ship missile about to strike a target vessel. (*ECPA*)

their operating frequency up and down the spectrum. Such diversity has so added to the complexities of signal identification and threat priorities that there are those who now question the future value of defensive EW.

But the US Navy, one of the world's most advanced users of EW technology, does not share this view, as indicated by its current countermeasures technology programme. The USN has been examining the whole of naval EW for at least the last four years, spending an estimated total of $107.9 million to fiscal year 1985. The programme is intended to support the development of "effective fleet countermeasures for use against hostile weapons systems designed for surveillance, C^3, target acquisition and weapons guidance". It includes developments right across the EW spectrum, from systems control through inflatable radar reflectors to mission-adaptable receiver systems, anti-radiation missile countermeasures and masking techniques for US shipborne radars. Perhaps the most interesting aspect of this whole vast enterprise is Project F34-375, which looked during FY-1982-83 at optical, infra-red, ultra-violet methods of detecting and classifying threats, and guiding and targeting friendly weapons. Such a move away from the radio-frequency portion of the electromagnetic spectrum could herald the end of naval EW as it is now known. But whatever the future may hold, EW remains fundamental to current naval activity.

Above: **The SCOT satellite communications antenna aboard the ill-fated HMS *Sheffield*. It is believed that at the time of the attack which led to her destruction her electronic surveillance systems, which would have warned of the missile's approach, were shut down to avoid interference with a transmission to Task Force headquarters. (*C. & S. Taylor*)**

Above right: **Aegis-equipped cruiser USS *Ticonderoga*. (*US Navy*)**

Right: **The operations room aboard a British Type 42 destroyer. The already onerous task of a naval commander in combat is further complicated by the demands of the electronic war. (*Plessey*)**

Sources and further reading

A wide range of open material has been consulted during the preparation of this article, including *Naval Radar* and *US Naval Weapons* by Norman Friedman (Conway Maritime Press, 1981 and 1983 respectively) and *The History of US Electronic Warfare: Vol 1* by Alfred Price (The Association of Old Crows, 1984). The following also contain further information on naval EW:

Jane's Weapon Systems edited by Ronald Pretty (Jane's Publishing Co) This annual database provides detailed information on current EW systems.

The Ships and Aircraft of the US Fleet by Norman Polmar (Arms & Armour Press, 1981, 12th edition) A useful survey of the US Navy and its equipment, containing brief details of EW equipment installed in USN ships and aircraft.

Guide to the Soviet Navy by Norman Polmar (Arms & Armour Press, 1983, 3rd edition) A survey giving brief details of the EW equipment carried by the Soviet Navy's ships and aircraft.

Anti-mine hovercraft: has their time come?

G. H. Elsey

Royal Navy BH.7 Mk 2 fitted with Plessey Type 193M sonar. (*BHC*)

Although the potential advantages of the hovercraft for mine countermeasures (MCM) were first realised more than 20 years ago, there are still no hovercraft in service in this role. Many studies and trials have been carried out, and in 1975 the British Inter-service Hovercraft Trials Unit was reformed as the Naval Hovercraft Trials Unit (NHTU) to evaluate the hovercraft in the MCM role. The trials probed the shock resistance, underwater signatures, towing capability and control characteristics of existing types, while the studies looked at their operational capability and produced designs for new craft. However, despite encouraging results and the enthusiastic support of NHTU, there was a general reluctance in naval circles to accept that hovercraft could effectively perform a task which has traditionally been performed by ships.

The hovercraft's speed and invulnerability are not in question, but doubts concerning seaworthiness, endurance and crew fatigue are frequently expressed.

The British Hovercraft Corporation (BHC) claims that such criticisms fail to take account of the technical advances made during the last few years. As a result, hovercraft can now tolerate far more severe sea states and offer significantly better payload and range.

Refinements in flexible skirt design have produced sizeable reductions in drag, particularly in rough water. At the same time, motion characteristics have been greatly improved. In addition, there are now becoming available gas turbine engines offering specific fuel consumption (sfc) 20–25% better than that of the previous generation, with a corresponding improvement in range and endurance.

The Hunt-class mine countermeasures vessel HMS *Chiddingfold*. (*Mike Lennon*)

The mining threat

Island nations like the UK, which are heavily dependent on shipping for their trade, are very vulnerable to mines. All the important commercial ports and military bases could be mined early in a war, rendering them unusable until the mines could be neutralised or at least located and marked.

Mines have become increasingly more sophisticated and now bear little resemblance to the moored devices which were common in the two world wars. Moored mines are still used, but are outnumbered by ground mines lying on the seabed. These weapons are actuated by a ship's acoustic, magnetic or pressure signature, or by a combination of all three. Some mines are actuated only after several passes, making them more difficult to sweep. There are also homing anti-submarine mines which can be laid in deep water.

Mines have numerous advantages for the aggressor, being relatively cheap, long-lived and difficult to locate and neutralise. They can also be laid surreptitiously by ships, submarines, hovercraft or aircraft. This makes it all the more likely that any future conflict will involve the use of mines.

The sweeping and hunting of mines has traditionally been performed by relatively small ships typified by the Royal Navy's "Ton"-class coastal minesweepers and the later "Hunt"-class MCMVs. Sweeping is

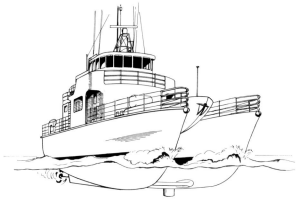

The conventional approach to mine countermeasures: Australia's Bay-class catamaran-hulled inshore minehunter (above), and HMS *Carron* (below), one of the Royal Navy's River-class minesweepers. (*Royal Navy*)

carried out by towing mechanical (wire) or influence (magnetic and/or acoustic) sweeps over the suspect area. Minehunting consists of locating mine-like objects with sonar, moving in closer to verify that the object is a mine, and finally disposing of it by placing an explosive charge nearby. The charge can be placed by divers working from a small dinghy, or more elegantly by a remotely controlled submersible.

This work is unavoidably dangerous when carried out by minesweeper ships, despite the use of wooden or GRP hulls, elaborate degaussing measures, and other measures. An MCM craft based on an amphibious hovercraft would significantly reduce the risks associated with such operations.

One of the most powerful arguments in favour of MCM hovercraft is their ability to tolerate underwater explosions. (*BHC*)

How is the hovercraft safer?

The amphibious hovercraft is a safer MCM platform on two counts: shock resistance and underwater signatures. Full-scale trials with several craft have convincingly shown that a hovercraft will withstand the underwater shock of a mine explosion at close quarters, and measurements have confirmed that the underwater magnetic, acoustic and pressure signatures are lower than those of conventional ships, and could be reduced still further by special design. And whereas a ship's acoustic signature deteriorates when it is manoeuvring, or if the screws are damaged, the hovercraft's can be kept constant.

Accurate positioning and control are also vital for MCM operations, and trials have shown that the control system of the BHC SR.N4 is more than adequate, the craft having been found capable of a higher standard of track-keeping accuracy than is expected from conventional ships.

A hovercraft can work effectively either by itself or in conjunction with conventional MCM vessels. The speed at which minehunting ships are able to move forward in a mined area is limited because they must check each contact. If it is a mine it has to be disposed of before the ship can safely proceed. A hovercraft, being less vulnerable, could perform a "precursory" survey, marking each contact and leaving the slower classification and disposal operations to a follow-up craft which could be either a hovercraft or a conventional MCMV. In this way it would be possible to identify a safe route, or one requiring a minimum of mine disposal work, more quickly than is possible with conventional MCM vessels alone.

Can a hovercraft carry the necessary equipment?

Hovercraft capable of carrying minehunting and minesweeping gear already exist. Over the last few years the British Ministry of Defence has funded design studies of the use of hovercraft in the MCM role, several of which have dealt specifically with the feasibility of fitting and deploying standard mine-sweeping and minehunting equipment. This work has shown that a large hovercraft similar to the SR.N4s used on commercial cross-Channel ferry services could carry, deploy and recover the same type of equipment as a modern MCM vessel. This includes:
● Plessey Type 193M hull sonar (deployed on a retractable tube)
● Remotely controlled mine disposal system (PAP 104 or similar) with magazine
● Full navigation and action information organisation (NAV/A10)
● Osborn acoustic sweep
● MM Mk 11 magnetic-loop influence sweep
● W Mk 3 wire sweep

It would be possible to carry all this equipment simultaneously on an SR.N4, allowing the craft to operate as a multi-role MCM craft, but endurance would be limited. A more effective approach would be to equip the craft for one specific role so that more fuel could be carried. For example, a minehunter/disposal

The Royal Navy's sole remaining hovercraft is BH.7 P235.

craft would need only the sonar, the mine disposal system and the NAV/A10, while a minesweeper version would carry only the sweep plus NAV/A10.

Interior space is ample and there is no difficulty in providing living accommodation for the crew, particularly as the complement of a hovercraft is generally smaller than that of a comparable ship. This is because the ship carries on-board maintenance personnel whereas all hovercraft maintenance is normally done ashore.

In 1982 BHC submitted to the Ministry of Defence a feasibility study of a 300-ton single-role minehunter based on the SR.N4 hovercraft. Directly competing were two similar studies, one based on a conventional ship, the other on the Tripartite minehunting system. The decision went against the hovercraft.

Operationally useful combinations of MCM equipment can also be carried by smaller craft. The Royal Navy's 55-ton BH.7 has carried out a wide range of MCM activities, including the towing of helicopter sweep gear and trials with a Plessey 193M minehunting sonar. Preliminary trials served to settle doubts about the effectiveness of sonar in the volume directly beneath a hovercraft. The same craft was later fitted with a fully operational minehunting fit and in 1983 completed a successful series of trials at Portland. The minehunting fit comprised a Plessey 193M sonar,

2048 Speedscan, Racal Positioning Systems QX1 navigation stack, and a Mk 20 plotting table, all of which are in current service with the Royal Navy. This exercise, including the design work and trials, was completed within nine months, thanks to a high degree of co-operation between the MoD, the Royal Navy and the companies.

Capabilities demonstrated during the trials included:
● Maximum detection and classification performance from the sonar in the conventional hunting role.
● Successful route survey operations using Speedscan at up to twice the speed of conventional ships.
● A full 360° azimuth field of view as a result of the absence of stern-arc propulsion noise.
● Improved track-keeping and hover accuracy compared with conventional minehunters.
● No degradation of the craft's underwater signature with the sonar tube immersed.

Currently under development are towed side-scanning sonars which can be operated at relatively high speeds and will permit fast route surveillance to be carried out routinely. The hovercraft is ideal for route surveillance, combining high speed with a high

SR.N6 Mk 6 pictured during trials with the Marconi 360° towed sonar. (*BHC*)

degree of invulnerability. Unlike a conventional ship, a hovercraft would be able to pass over mines at low risk to itself and with a good chance of surviving the explosion if one were detonated. Helicopters are the only other vehicles likely to be able to tow high-speed sonar equipment effectively.

It is possible that for shallow-water operations quite small minehunting sonars, capable of being deployed by correspondingly smaller craft, will be developed. A move in this direction is the Marconi 360° sonar, which has been deployed from the 16-ton SR.N6 Mk 6.

Seakeeping and habitability

Many of the misconceptions about the seakeeping characteristics of hovercraft stem from the problems of earlier types, which resulted from insufficient development of the flexible skirts and attempts to operate in areas for which smaller craft were unsuitable. Seakeeping ability is to a large extent dependent on size, particularly length, and becomes a severe restraint if too small a craft is chosen for a particular job. While small hovercraft like the SR.N6 have shown an impressive capability for their size in areas such as the Falklands, effective minehunting or sweeping in

adverse sea states without undue discomfort to the crew requires a craft of adequate size.

Exactly how large depends on what is expected operationally, but the performance of the SR.N4s on the cross-Channel routes serves to illustrate the seakeeping capability of a 200–300-ton craft. Having started operations in 1968, the six craft have accumulated many thousands of running hours and the operational limits have gradually been extended.

In trials to achieve CAA approval to operate with farepaying passengers the SR.N4 Mk 3 (Super 4) has demonstrated adequate control in severe conditions – up to 7m significant wave height and 50kt mean windspeed. Only a very small percentage of scheduled Channel crossings are cancelled due to the weather. Bearing in mind that minehunting or minesweeping gear is unlikely to be capable of operating in extreme seas, it can be argued that an MCM hovercraft need be no larger than the SR.N4 series.

Motion characteristics are also important to crew efficiency, and again favourable comparisons with conventional MCM vessels can be drawn. The roll motion of an SR.N4 is about half that of a "Ton"-class vessel in a comparable sea state, while pitch amplitudes and bow vertical accelerations are fairly similar. Analysis of vertical acceleration measurements has indicated that seasickness is unlikely to be a problem in a large hovercraft, either during the high-speed transit or in the low-speed minehunting phase.

Endurance

As with all transport vehicles, maximum endurance is achieved when the weight of fuel carried is maximised and the power and fuel consumption minimised. This means that for a given size of craft the characteristics necessary for high endurance are:
- A high disposable load/all-up-weight ratio
- A low power/weight ratio
- Low-sfc engines

The hovercraft's efficient structure results in a disposable load normally equal to about 40% of its all-up weight in a typical civil configuration. But in a military craft it is possible to increase this to better than 55% by stripping out unnecessary furnishings and equipment. The buoyancy-tank raft structure could accommodate all this weight as fuel.

Developments in hovercraft technology, particularly relating to the skirts, have greatly reduced the power/weight ratio. While earlier types required 90 or 100hp per ton, the Super 4 needs only 50. At the same time, the Super 4 also offers substantially improved sea state capability.

The BH.7 and SR.N4 series are fitted with Proteus gas turbines which, though having proved themselves reliable over many thousands of operating hours, are undeniably thirsty in comparison with newer power-plants. Typically, a modern gas turbine achieves an sfc of 0.5lb/hp/hr or less, compared with about 0.65 for the Proteus, representing a potential improvement of nearly 25%. The modern gas turbine also retains its low sfc over a wider power output range, an advantage for roles like minehunting, in which a large proportion of the operating time is spent at low power.

Recent studies have shown that re-engining the SR.N4 and increasing its all-up weight and fuel tankage would yield endurances of several days in the very-low-speed minehunting mode. The corresponding ferry range would exceed 2,000 miles.

Base requirements

All maintenance work on amphibious hovercraft is normally done ashore, although if necessary some servicing could be carried out alongside a jetty or at a mooring. For repairs and maintenance of the skirt a simple base taking the form of a hardstanding and clear access to the sea is required. A fleet of military hovercraft could be operated satisfactorily from mobile forward support units backed up by one or more main bases possessing facilities for major repairs and maintenance.

Recent craft developments

BH.7 Improved versions of the BH.7 in which the Proteus is replaced by an Allison 571K gas turbine have been projected over the last few years. This engine produces significantly more power than the Proteus at a lower sfc. Together with the technological improvements which have taken place since the BH.7 was originally designed, this permits large increases in disposable load, all-up weight and endurance.

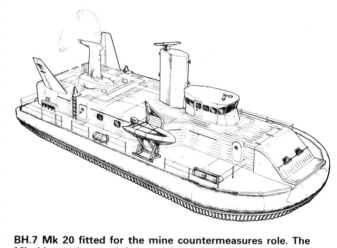

BH.7 Mk 20 fitted for the mine countermeasures role. The Mk 20 can be used for a variety of other military roles, including amphibious assault, anti-submarine warfare and fast attack. (*BHC*)

The latest BH.7 development is the Mk 20, which at 94 tons AUW has a disposable load of 40 tons – more than double that of the earlier marks. The hull is lengthened by 24ft to increase the interior space while retaining the cutaway forward side cabins of the Mk 5, which provide useful deck space for mounting weapons and other equipment. Equipped as a mine-hunter, the Mk 20 could remain on station for 30hr operating at 2–5kt in the search mode, or 15hr at 10–12kt in the Speedscan mode. Both endurances assume a distance from base of 100nm.

The BH.7 Mk 20 is also suitable for a number of other military roles, including logistic support/amphibious assault, anti-submarine warfare and fast attack.

SR.N4

The SR.N4 has been developed in its civil form from the 170-ton Mk 1, through the 200-ton Mk 2, to the Mk 3 or Super 4, which is stretched by seven structural bays and operates at an AUW of over 300 tons. The MCMH version is capable of operating at 330 tons AUW and again benefits from the higher power and better sfc of Allison turbines. This craft has a disposable load of approximately 190 tons, plus a vastly increased fuel tankage enabling it to undertake sorties of several days' duration in the low-speed minehunting role.

Although heavier than the Super 4, the MCMH version is based on the unstretched Mk 2 platform, mainly to minimise its cost. The more powerful engines and deeper, low-pressure Super 4-type skirt enable the MCMH to achieve speed and motion characteristics closer to those of the Super 4 despite its lesser length and increased cushion pressure.

An MCMH based on the Super 4 platform would be even more satisfactory. The allowable AUW would be about 500 tons, with a corresponding further increase in disposable load to nearly 300 tons. This could be exploited in the form of more equipment or additional fuel.

AP.1-88

The latest craft to be produced by the British Hovercraft Corporation, the AP.1-88 was designed as a passenger ferry but also has potential as an MCM craft. It differs from the company's other hovercraft in having a welded structure and diesel engines, features which help to reduce both building and maintenance costs. AP.1-88 is 80ft long and has a maximum AUW of 40 tons.

Preliminary studies have shown that it would be feasible to install Type 193M sonar in an AP.1-88, particularly if the craft was lengthened to increase the disposable load and interior space.

SR.N4 Mk 3 operated on cross-Channel services. Craft of this size would be needed for minehunting sorties lasting several days. (*BHC*)

The hovercraft currently available have a minehunting capability which, with development, could comfortably improve on that of comparable ships. They also show great promise for the route surveillance role, which is expected to become increasingly important in the future and which only a hovercraft or a helicopter is likely to be able to perform at high speed and with an acceptable degree of risk.

The AP.1-88, latest product of the British Hovercraft Corporation. Originally designed as a passenger ferry, the AP.1-88 could be stretched to accommodate the Plessey Type 193M sonar. (*BHC*)

AEGIS shoots down the critics

Adm James D. Watkins USN

USS *Vincennes*, third of 12 cruisers of the AEGIS-equipped *Ticonderoga* class, fires a live missile during sea trials in spring 1985. (*Litton/Ingalls Shipbuilding*)

The AEGIS multi-target air-defence and command system and its first platform, the USS *Ticonderoga* (CG-47), came of age together in April 1984 when the cruiser completed her first deployment, to the Mediterranean off the Lebanon, and subsequent tactical missile firings off Puerto Rico. In doing so the ship had fired more than 80 surface-to-air missiles, nine ASROC anti-submarine rockets, six over-the-side torpedoes, three Harpoon surface-to-surface missiles and more than 1,400 rounds of 5/54 ammunition. She had handled more than 500 helicopter movements to and from her helicopter deck and carried out more than 3,000 intercepts with aircraft under her control

in fleet exercises. Most important of all, she had clearly demonstrated the ability of AEGIS to act as a force multiplier in battle group operations.

Before this deployment *Ticonderoga* had proved her ability to detect, in heavy jamming conditions, all targets attacking a battle group, even those not detected by other ships. In missile exercises with cruisers, destroyers and frigates *Ticonderoga* showed several of the other ships how to acquire and engage the targets effectively. She was thus able to get the most out of the battle group's surface-to-air missile assets, conserving her own missiles for only the most demanding targets.

The Lebanon deployment provided several opportunities to demonstrate *Ticonderoga*'s seaworthiness and manoeuvrability. In high sea states during her Atlantic crossing and the rough water of a Mediterranean winter her handling and seaworthiness proved to be of the highest calibre. She carried out sustained high-speed transits, proceeded smartly with USS *Independence* to reach operational areas off the Lebanon, and handled all high-speed and manoeuvring commitments with ease. If rough weather can ever be considered a pleasure, her crew were glad to encounter rough conditions so that they could put the ship through her manoeuvrability paces and thus clearly refute criticisms of her seaworthiness.

Operating off the Lebanon from November 1983 to March 1984, *Ticonderoga* impressively demonstrated her air-defence system, the world's most advanced. The AEGIS SPY-1 radar provided the most comprehensive air picture ever seen in the eastern Mediterranean, controlled all air activities in *Ticonderoga*'s area and permitted a dramatic reduction in carrier combat air patrol launches, thus saving about $1 million per day in fuel costs.

She also served as the platform for the anti-air warfare commander during the deployment, allowing him to manage the entire air picture rather than simply reacting to it. AEGIS was able to track all contacts within 250 miles and to detect small, low-flying targets and aircraft coming off the land and out of mountain regions. That capability created a great deal of peace of mind in an area where commercial and private aircraft of all sizes might have proved to be a terrorist threat and had to be detected early and tracked constantly.

The robustness of AEGIS was demonstrated magnificently as the system remained 100% available over more than four months. This high degree of

---

USS *Ticonderoga* in company with the battleship *New Jersey* off the Lebanese coast in 1984.

operational readiness, coupled with sound radar performance and comprehensive air-defence displays, gave the battle group commander a new dimension in anti-air security. The constant availability of AEGIS permitted *Ticonderoga* to pass her tactical picture continuously to the carrier and other battle-group ships, giving them the benefit of the SPY-1 radar's comprehensive detection and surveillance coverage. Complementing AEGIS were the carrierborne E-2C Hawkeye early-warning aircraft, which extended the target-detection umbrella still further. Finally, *Ticonderoga* proved able to keep her air-defence guard well up even while conducting naval gunfire support operations off Beirut.

Since no actual missiles were fired in the Mediterranean, *Ticonderoga* diverted to Puerto Rico for tactical missile firings before returning to the continental United States. Rear Admiral Edward W. Carter III, Commander Test and Evaluation Force (COMOPTEVFOR) and the Navy's independent evaluator, carried out the most extensive tests ever on a surface combatant. The varied and demanding target profiles included high, medium and low-altitude

presentations, with several sea-skimmer (Exocet) profiles being simulated. Multiple raids by subsonic and supersonic target aircraft, plus dense wartime jamming and chaff, were thrown at the ship. Safety permitting, all of the tests were as warlike as possible, with realistic target profiles and tactics. Afterwards Rear Admiral Carter remarked: "*Ticonderoga* destroyed ten of 11 targets (hard-warhead kills requiring no further evaluation) presented in an operational environment, achieving a kill effectiveness of 91%. Target presentations included sea-skimmers and a Harpoon ASM in a clear environment and simultaneous multiple targets in heavy jamming and chaff. *Ticonderoga* has come of age since we last tested her. Her crew is solidly professional, her systems virtually flawless, and her tactical doctrine is sound. The threats which we threw at her represented the maximum effort which we are capable of generating at this time. She ate them up effortlessly. Tough as they

Below: **Recent AEGIS deployments include Exercise BALTOPS 85, held in the Baltic in October 1985. USS *Ticonderoga* is in the centre of the picture, with the battleship *Iowa* off her port side. (*US Navy*)**

Right: **USS *Yorktown*, second of class and survivor of severe shock tests that caused minor damage but left the SPY-1 radar fully operational.**

were, our tests did not begin to approach what we believe to be CG-47's ultimate capability."

Through actual missile firings off Puerto Rico, during *Ticonderoga*'s maiden Sixth Fleet deployment and in several battle group exercises, the AEGIS system's basic characteristics of fast reaction time, jam-resistance, total coverage (high and low-altitude targets), firepower and reliability have been demonstrated amply. Her commissioning commanding officer and skipper on her maiden deployment said: "Our deployment and the varied tasks which we had to support further enhanced our appreciation for the new warfighting dimensions which AEGIS possesses. It was ironic to read of concerns being expressed back home as to our safety off Lebanon. We could not have been more safe. Be if off Lebanon with the constant threat of terrorist and missile attacks or off Puerto Rico in warlike Follow-on Test and Evaluation (FOT&E) tests, there is no more capable ship in the world to handle the cruise missile threat. If we had to go into harm's way, there is not (another) ship in the world that I would prefer being on."

Two sister ships – USS *Yorktown* (CG-48) and *Vincennes* (CG-49) – have now joined the fleet. *Yorktown* has already demonstrated the robustness of AEGIS and her ability to endure and fight during shock tests conducted in August 1984. AEGIS performed reliably throughout, even after the most severe underwater shock. The heart of the weapon system, the SPY-1 radar, remained operational. Minor damage to various systems was predicted and did occur. The ship's crew was however able to restore lost capabilities promptly, and the ship's warfighting capacity remained intact throughout.

The addition to the AEGIS cruiser of LAMPS Mk III helicopters, as embarked in *Vincennes*, and vertical launching systems (VLS), to be introduced in *Bunker Hill* (CG-52) in September 1986, promises to give the US Navy an even broader multi-warfare capability and an opportunity to keep ahead of the threat. The men who sail these ships consider that they would truly have the edge in combat. They marvel at the performance they can achieve, and are proving every day that the loudly expressed doubts about AEGIS performance have no foundation in truth.

With the AEGIS-equipped *Arleigh Burke* (DDG-51) class due to join the fleet in 1989, the US Navy is continuing to improve the quality of its battle forces and to acquire the numbers needed to give this formidable new warfighting capacity a truly global dimension.

The SH-60B Seahawk LAMPS III anti-submarine helicopter is now embarked in USS *Vincennes*, adding advanced ASW to an already impressive array of capabilities. (*Sikorsky*)

Artist's impression of the first vertical-launch-capable AEGIS cruiser, USS *Bunker Hill*, and (behind) the destroyer *Arleigh Burke*, first of a new class. (*RCA*)

NATO's naval problems: severe but surmountable

Dr J. M. Luns

The extreme importance of the NATO navies to a successful defence of the territories covered by the Alliance is universally acknowledged. A superficial look at the forces suggests that the situation is on the whole not unsatisfactory. There is first of all the enormous and very impressive navy of the United States of America. Britain and France – a likely ally though not a formal member of the alliance – possess important naval capabilities, and the oceangoing navies of Italy, the Federal Republic of Germany, the Netherlands and Spain represent a significant contribution to NATO's strength. Although belonging in this category the Canadian Navy is, in view of the vast coastline of that country, significantly undersized.

The European NATO escort force compares well with that of the Soviet Navy, totalling about 250 ships in service plus over 50 more building or authorised. This is the new Dutch anti-aircraft frigate *Jacob van Heemskerck*. (*Royal Netherlands Navy*)

Lastly there are the navies of the other European allies – Turkey, Greece, Portugal, Norway, Denmark and Belgium – which are mainly meant for the defence of their home waters. Together all these navies do indeed present an impressive armada, one not too inferior in some categories to the Red Fleet. One important exception is the submarine component, an area in which the Soviet Union is vastly superior.

Soviet submarine strength is far superior to that of NATO, even when the French force – not formally committed to the Alliance – is included. This is the *Agosta*-class patrol submarine *Ouessant*.

After hitting a low point in the mid-1970s, Western carrier strength is slowly recovering. The Italian Navy's *Giuseppe Garibaldi* may eventually embark Sea Harriers.

Naval strength of the European NATO allies

Category	Number
Submarines	
Ballistic (nuclear)	10 (5)
Attack (nuclear)	16 (10)
Oceangoing	59 (31)
Coastal	46
Aircraft carriers	8
Helicopter carriers	2
Cruisers	3
Destroyers/large frigates	101 (11)
Frigates	154 (42)
Corvettes	34 (12)
Fast attack craft	
Missile	130 (20)
Torpedo	34
Minelayers	8
MCM ships	51 (46)
Minesweepers	161 (26)
Assault ships	4 (4)
Fast combat support ships	26 (4)
Patrol craft, tankers, supply ships, large tugs, etc	more than 400

( ) = building or authorised.

Although, as shown above, in number and quality of ships the European NATO navies constitute an important addition to US naval strength, it would be over-optimistic to conclude that there is no room for improvement. For one thing, in naval warfare the aggressor enjoys advantages which he does not have in the land battle.

Firstly, the great mobility of ships allows the aggressor to concentrate superior strength in a chosen sector. Thus the small German surface fleet tied down a great number of Allied, but mainly British, major naval units for a long period during the last war.

Secondly, NATO has to protect a great quantity of merchant shipping, resulting in a weakening of its forces. And it is not only the ships in the North Atlantic that have to be covered, but also those sailing round the Cape and in the Indian Ocean and South Atlantic.

Lastly, in war the Soviet Union would not have to rely on the oceans for its supplies of essential materials, which could be obtained either from its own territories or in the neighbouring communist countries. NATO, on the other hand, would be absolutely dependent on a free flow of troops, military material and vital

Federal Germany's small but efficient escort force would play a useful part in the protection of reinforcement shipping. *Hessen*, pictured here, and her sisters of the *Hamburg* class are due to be replaced by either the NATO Type 90 frigate or the German Type 124 destroyer. (*Federal German Navy*)

commodities like oil from America, the Middle East and other regions. Strong Soviet squadrons comprising aircraft carriers, heavy and light cruisers, and powerful frigates would threaten this traffic. More formidable a menace still is the huge Soviet submarine fleet. Compared with nuclear ballistic and attack submarines and even modern conventional boats, the German submarines of the Second World War were of negligible value. And yet they nearly succeeded in cutting the lifeline between America and the UK, which might have forced the British to capitulate. Of course certain potent, anti-submarine weapons, such as homing torpedoes and missiles, did not exist during the last war, and the whole range of ASW measures have been vastly improved since then, but even so submarines have become steadily more sophisticated and dangerous than the forces opposing them.

The NATO admirals are therefore right when they express concern about the Soviet naval threat and when they try to induce the NATO governments to expand their maritime forces. NATO does however have some

Set a sub to catch a sub: Western nuclear attack boats like the French *Saphir* would be tasked principally with operations against their Soviet counterparts. (*DTCN*)

strategic advantages of its own, for instance, geography is on the side of the West because of the very unfavourable configuration of the Soviet coastline. This means that the Soviet Navy has had to be divided into four fleets covering the four seas adjoining the USSR: the Northern, the Baltic, the Black Sea and the North Pacific.

The Northern Sea offers the best outlet to the open oceans, but there is only one ice-free harbour, Murmansk, and this is vulnerable to air attacks from Norway and Iceland and from the Allied fleets deployed between the two. Iceland's membership of NATO is a great advantage, giving the Alliance an enormous unsinkable aircraft carrier stationed at just the right place. The Baltic has a very difficult exit through Danish and Norwegian waters, and the many infringements of Swedish territorial waters by Soviet submarines in recent years clearly show the nervousness of the Soviet naval command about the dangers to their ships in this region, where they would be exposed to attacks from the Federal German Navy and Allied aircraft. The Soviets are clearly seeking a safe passage through Swedish waters for their ships, especially their submarines.

The Black Sea has the most difficult outlet of all, and in war the Bosphorus, Sea of Marmara and the Dardanelles would form a formidable obstacle for Soviet warships and shipping. It is therefore to be expected that in time of acute international tension

there would be a substantial increase in the number of Soviet warships passing through on their way to the Mediterranean to take up war stations.

Finally, in the Far East the Soviet fleets are concentrated mainly at Vladivostok. It is thus reassuring that Japan, linked to the United States by a bilateral military treaty, has in recent years expanded her navy. This is once again a significant factor in the Far East, though it should be expanded further. On a recent visit to the huge Japanese naval base at Yokosuka I was impressed by the discipline and smart appearance of the Japanese officers and men, and by the excellent condition of their ships. It is highly probable that Japan would be on the side of the allies if ever a new world conflict was to erupt.

NATO's second major advantage is the fact that – for the first time in the history of military alliances – its forces are largely integrated into a joint defence plan. On the naval side, a common command structure and planning, and regular Alliance-wide manoeuvres, mean that in war the various fleets would work together effectively right from the start.

Above: **Even the Soviet trawler fleet must be regarded as part of the USSR's naval strength. Working trawlers like *Geroi Adzhimushkaya*, seen here in the English Channel, usually carry intelligence-gathering equipment and include military personnel in their crews. (*Royal Navy*)**

Below: **NATO is steadily improving its ability to respond to the mine-warfare threat. France, Belgium and the Netherlands are building significant numbers of the Tripartite minehunter/sweeper design. This is *Eridan*, first of a fleet of ten for the French Navy. (*L. & L. van Ginderen*)**

European NATO cruisers like the Italian *Caio Duilio* would represent a powerful addition to any convoy escort force. (*Marius Bar*)

To complete the picture, we should consider the merchant navies, particularly that of the Soviet Union. The USSR's huge merchant navy (about 32 million tons, including the tonnage of Poland, Romania and Bulgaria), fishing fleets and research vessels are under strict central command, and even in peacetime are tasked with supporting the Soviet Navy on the high seas. They are also used for spying on the NATO navies. Formidable though it is, however, the Soviet merchant marine is far smaller than the combined NATO fleets, which would have a far greater role to play in war.

The wartime tasks of NATO's maritime forces are manifold. They would act as the first line of defence, resisting incursions into the North Norwegian coastal waters and closing the Baltic exits and the entrance to the Mediterranean from the Black Sea. In the Mediterranean a strong American naval squadron will be a powerful supplement to the navies of France, Italy, Spain, Greece and Turkey, so much so that the Soviet Navy could suffer serious setbacks in these waters. Moreover, the Straits of Gibraltar form a nearly impossible passage for hostile surface vessels.

Another major challenge to the European navies would be the countering of the very impressive Soviet mine warfare capability. Apart from clearing the coastal seas, they would have to keep open and free from mines the entrances to the main ports of Great Britain and of the Continent, particularly Hamburg, Rotterdam, Antwerp, Brest and Le Havre. Here the picture is far from reassuring, with NATO's MCM

and minesweeper forces being far too small to have any chance of performing their mission successfully. As a result, large numbers of auxiliary minesweepers would have to be drawn from the fishing fleets and rapidly converted. At the same time, the NATO navies would be fighting an anti-submarine campaign of unparallelled intensity and difficulty.

Finally, there would be convoy duties in the Mediterranean, the North Sea and Danish-Norwegian coastal waters. The oceangoing components of the European navies – the carriers, cruisers and large missile-carrying frigates, and nuclear and non-coastal conventional submarines – would join the American and Canadian navies in protecting convoys coming from the United States and the Middle East, as well as contributing a modest but real reinforcement to the US task forces.

The balance of naval forces in Europe remains far from reassuring. But there is no reason to be despondent, because NATO possesses strong navies and some vital advantages. And the tremendous industrial and shipbuilding capabilities of the United States make it reasonable to expect that even after some initial setbacks NATO would be able to contain and beat off the assaults of the Soviet Navy.

Latin American navies: living beyond their means

Adrian English

Uruguayan patrol craft **Comodoro Coe** of the **Vigilante** class.

Latin America controls both major means of access between the Atlantic and Pacific oceans, via the Panama Canal at the north of the South American continent and Cape Horn at its southern tip. The Falklands War focused international attention on the strategic importance of this region, and the continuing strife in Central America keeps it fixed there. Although the region had hitherto been regarded as a strategic backwater, its major nations have always boasted respectable navies, sometimes equipped with extremely sophisticated material. In spite of the debt crisis which to varying degrees afflicts all Latin American countries, the major regional powers and some aspiring second-rank nations strive to continue this tradition.

Argentina, Brazil, Chile and Peru, known collectively as the "ABCP" powers, have traditionally been the major military and naval nations in Latin America. They currently remain so, though the pecking order

of their navies has changed over the years. Chile, originally the major naval power in the region, has fallen to fourth place, with Peru now third and lagging behind Argentina and Brazil in lacking embarked air power. These two nations, both of which remain members of the increasingly exclusive club of operators of traditional aircraft carriers are closely matched. Argentina perhaps possesses the edge by virtue of the number and modernity of its major surface combatants, which balance Brazil's larger but mainly obsolete submarine force.

Peru is Latin America's undisputed leader in submarines, both qualitatively and quantitatively, and also possesses an impressive if largely obsolete surface

Above: **Peruvian Type 1200 patrol submarine *Antofagasta*.**

Right: *La Argentina* (foreground) and *Almirante Brown*, two of Argentina's four MEKO 360 destroyers. (*Blohm und Voss*)

fleet. But although the Chilean Navy's personnel still have more expertise than those of any other naval force in the region, it has suffered to an almost catastrophic extent from the effects of the international boycott which followed the overthrow of the Marxist regime of Salvador Allende in 1973.

Venezuela, Colombia and Ecuador lag well behind the big four, with an outsider, Fidel Castro's Cuba, probably possessing the most potent naval force in the Caribbean after that of the United States itself. The remaining naval forces of the region, including Mexico's numerous coastal patrol fleet, have limited to negligible combat potential.

The "ABCP" powers

The Argentinian Navy has now more than made good the losses suffered in the Falklands War of 1982. All four MEKO 360 destroyers are now in service, together with the first two of the six projected MEKO 140 corvettes. Two more MEKO 140s are close to completion, though work on the last pair has slowed down. The three French-built A69 light frigates complete a relatively impressive and modern escort/missile-strike force. The navy seems to have resisted successfully pressures from the civilian government for the disposal of two MEKO 360s and two 140s, although the two Type 42 destroyers remain on the sales list, with no apparent takers.

The first two of the six projected TR 1700 submarines have joined two Type 209 boats in what remains a fairly modest submarine force; there is no immediate sign of the four additional Type 1700s materialising. The rumour of the purchase of a French nuclear submarine appears to be without foundation, and the possible ultimate completion of the four remaining Type 1700s to a modified design with nuclear propulsion seems to be equally unlikely.

Although decidedly long in the tooth, the carrier *Veinticinco de Mayo* soldiers on and now operates Super Etendards, the total number of which is rumoured to be 24 rather than the 14 originally ordered. The losses of Macchi MB.339s (one of which gave the coup de grace to HMS *Ardent*) during the Falklands War have been more than made good with the acquisition of 11 EMB.326 Xavantes from Brazil. Though the air force blocked the acquisition of 24 replacement Skyhawks from Israel, the navy now has an effective long-range maritime patrol/AEW capability in the form of six converted Lockheed Electras to complement its fair existing ASW force of six Grumman Trackers and four Sea Kings.

Though elderly, the Argentinian carrier *Veinticinco de Mayo* embarks an effective air wing centred on a squadron of Super Etendard strike aircraft. (*Dr Robert Scheina*)

Niteroi, first of a class of six frigates produced for Brazil by Vosper Thornycroft. (*C. & S. Taylor*)

The marines, who acquitted themselves well in the Falklands, have also acquired new equipment, including quantities of French ERC-90 armoured cars. Sealift remains inadequate, however, with only one elderly LST in service and another under construction.

The superficially larger Brazilian Navy includes seven submarines, although only the three *Oberon*s are of modern construction and the two projected Type 209 boats are proving slow to materialise. Ten obsolete ex-USN Second World War destroyers form the bulk of a relatively numerous but antiquated escort force, the only modern elements of which are the six Vosper-designed *Niterói*-class frigates. Only two of these carry surface-to-surface missiles. Two out of a projected total of 12 locally designed missile corvettes are building at a leisurely rate. The training ship *Brasil*, in effect a modified *Niterói*-class vessel, was completed in 1985.

The conversion of the venerable *Minas Gerais* into an attack carrier appears to have been delayed by the perennial rivalry between the Brazilian Navy and Air Force. Anachronistically, the latter operates all fixed-wing naval aircraft, and consequently Brazilian naval aviation lags far behind that of Argentina. Brazil's large and well-equipped marine corps, with four attack transports and two LSTs, is a little better off than that of Argentina when it comes to sealift and amphibious assault capacity.

Since the mid-1960s the Peruvian Navy has grown enormously, though largely through the purchase of obsolete material, notably from the Netherlands. The submarine force is nevertheless comparatively impressive, totalling six Type 209s and six elderly US-built boats.

The main strength of Peru's surface fleet lies in its four *Lupo*-class frigates and its six French-built missile attack craft; two elderly but modernised British *Daring*-class destroyers also mount SSMs. More impressive than potentially useful are the two ex-Netherlands cruisers *Almirante Grau* and *Aguirre*, the latter of which can carry three Sea King helicopters. The eight ex-Netherlands destroyers acquired over the last six years are expensive in manpower while being of only limited value in modern combat conditions.

Peru's modest marine corps has sufficient sealift capacity in the form of two transports, two LSTs and two LSMs, although the amphibious vessels date from the Second World War. Peruvian naval aviation is adequate in the areas of maritime patrol and ASW but lacks a strike element.

The Chilean Navy, Latin America's finest, has fallen on hard times. Its equipment shortcomings have been alleviated only to a degree by the acquisition of two British *County*-class missile destroyers which, together with the two 25-year-old Almirante-class vessels and two *Leander*-class frigates, form the backbone of its

Peruvian *Lupo*-class frigate launches an Otomat anti-ship missile.

The Chilean Navy is equipped largely with British ships, several of them transferred from the Royal Navy or Royal Fleet Auxiliary. This is the fleet tanker *Almirante Jorge Montt*, formerly *Tidepool*. (L. & L. van Ginderen)

surface fleet. A small but modern submarine arm comprises two *Oberon*s and two Type 209s.

The remainder of the surface fleet consists of the ancient if well preserved cruiser *O'Higgins*, the last "Washington Treaty" cruiser afloat and sister ship of Argentina's ill-fated *General Belgrano*, the elderly Swedish-built cruiser *Latorre* and two ex-US World War II destroyers. Two Israeli *Reshef*-class missile boats and four Spanish-built torpedo attack craft form a useful but quite inadequate coastal strike force.

The Chilean Marines are short of amphibious assault capability, having just five landing craft in the 300/800-ton range. Chile's naval aviation, like that of Peru, is primarily a maritime patrol/ASW force, the resources of which must be tightly stretched along the country's 4,000-mile coastline.

The secondary powers

The "Bolívar" countries – Columbia, Ecuador and Venezuela – maintain useful naval forces, with Venezuela's being the most impressive.

The main striking force of the Venezuelan Navy comprises six *Lupo*-class frigates and two Type 209 submarines. Surprisingly, the six *Constitución*-class fast attack craft, two of which carry SSMs, have been transferred to the new coastguard. Also transferred were the two surviving Italian-built *Almirante Clemente*-class destroyer escorts, which although recently modernised are almost 30 years old. The US Second World War submarine *Picúa* remains in service after a major refit in 1979–80. The relatively large and extremely well equipped marine corps is well served for sealift and amphibious assault capability by a transport, four new Korean-built LSTs, a Second World War-vintage landing ship and two 400-ton landing craft. The navy's aircraft form an adequate maritime patrol and ASW force.

The Ecuadorian Navy has recently received an important reinforcement in the form of six Italian-built *Esmeraldas*-class missile corvettes. Two Type 209 submarines and six missile attack craft complete the major sting of this small but well balanced force. Of less obvious value are the ex-US Second World War destroyer *Presidente Alfaro* and the troop transport *Morán Valverde*, although the latter does supplement the sealift and amphibious assault capacity provided for Ecuador's three marine battalions by a Second World War-vintage LST and two LSMs. Ecuadorean naval aviation is primarily a transport force, lacking adequate maritime patrol and ASW capability.

Although Colombia is the largest and most populous of the three Bolívar republics, with coastlines on both the Pacific and the Caribbean, her navy lags behind those of both Venezuela and Ecuador. The four

recently delivered Type FS 1500 missile frigates represent a valuable addition to a striking force hitherto limited to two Type 209 submarines commissioned in 1975. The elderly Swedish-built destroyer *Siete de Agosto* remains in service, although no attempt has been made to modernise its armament. The two recently acquired US *Asheville*-class gun-armed fast attack craft provide a limited coastal strike capability. The Colombian Navy has no amphibious assault or sealift capability whatsoever for its 2,500 marines, although the two Italian-built miniature submarines *Intrépido* and *Indomable* are designed for the delivery of attack swimmers. A small naval air arm, so far equipped only with four MBB BO105 helicopters and a few light fixed-wing aircraft, is being formed.

Venezuelan *Lupo*-class frigate *General Urdaneta*. (*Royal Netherlands Navy*)

Exocet-armed *Quito*-class fast attack craft of the Ecuadorian Navy.

The Caribbean cauldron

The Caribbean is currently Latin America's major flashpoint, the powder keg having already ignited in Central America. President Reagan of the United States has defined the latter region as the major battleground between democracy and communism, although the current role of the US Government in supporting resistance to the democratically elected if unpalatably left-of-centre government of Nicaragua rather belies this claim.

Mexico maintains a large but generally obsolete coastal patrol force which is significantly lacking in combat capability. The navy of the Dominican Republic has declined from its peak under the dictator Trujillo during the 1950s, when it was the most potent naval force in the Caribbean, and those of both the Central American republics and the former British colonies in the Caribbean are insignificant inshore patrol forces. Although still largely a coastal defence

Colombian Type FS 1500 frigate *Almirante Padilla*.

Koni-class frigate *Mariel* of the Cuban Navy.

force, the Cuban Revolutionary Navy overshadows all the others in this region in combat capability and seems destined to spread its influence wider following the recent establishment of a submarine arm.

The three Soviet Foxtrot-class conventionally-powered attack submarines known to have been delivered form the main long-range strike arm of the Cuban Navy. A single Whiskey-class boat is used primarily for training but could also act as a commando or guerrilla carrier. Backbone of the costal defence force is formed by 18 Osa and five Komar-class missile boats, constituting the largest missile boat force in Latin America. They are backed up by 13 torpedo boats and nine gun-armed attack hydrofoils. Main task of the two Koni-class light frigates so far delivered is apparently to act as command vessels for the coastal patrol and attack flotillas. The Soviets would appear to have deliberately limited the amphibious assault capacity of the Revolutionary Navy's small marine corps to two 800-ton LSMs, so limiting its role to that of a raiding force rather than a serious amphibious assault element. The Revolutionary Air Force provides an adequate maritime patrol force, plus a helicopter-based ASW capability which is harder to assess.

Despite its size and growing politico-economic importance, Mexico has traditionally relied implicitly on the United States for its defence, its own armed forces and in particular its navy being limited to little more than a police role. Although the discovery of vast

Matias de Cordova, an Azteca-class patrol boat operated by the Mexican Navy.

oil reserves in the mid-1970s appeared to have prompted a reassessment of the role of the Mexican armed forces, the modest expansion launched towards the close of the decade rapidly ran out of steam as the foreign debt crisis began to bite ever deeper.

The Mexican Navy remains a coastal patrol force, a role for which its numerical strength seems adequate. The only modern elements are the six *Halcón*-class exclusive economic zone (EEZ) patrol vessels built in Spain during the early 1980s, and the 31 units so far completed out of a projected total of 36 *Azteca*-class

patrol craft. The navy's major vessels are two ex-US Second World War destroyers, a destroyer escort of similar vintage, four troop transports and 36 ex-US *Auk* and *Admirable*-class minesweepers, all employed as patrol vessels and with minesweeping gear removed. There are also about two dozen inshore patrol craft and the ancient Spanish-built gunboats *Durango* and *Guanajuato*, both dating from the mid-1930s.

Apart from the troop transports, sealift capacity for the Mexican Marine Corps amounts to no more than two old US LSTs. Given that this unimpressive naval force must be divided between the Gulf and Pacific coasts, with a combined length of almost 5,800 miles, the modesty of the Mexican Navy and its almost total lack of combat capability appear all the more marked. The small naval air arm is adequate for the patrol of the Pacific coast, where most of its elements are deployed, but otherwise it is mainly a transport and training force lacking any combat or significant ASW capability.

The once proud Dominican Navy is now reduced in effect to a single 40-year-old Canadian River-class frigate and two similarly venerable US PCE-type corvettes in addition to less than a dozen inshore patrol craft, a few armed tugs and three former US *Cohoes*-class netlayers converted into patrol vessels. Sealift capacity for the small Dominican Marine Corps is effectively confined to a single ancient LSM, while the withdrawal of the Dominican Air Force's two Catalinas means that no effective airborne patrol or ASW capacity remains.

Of the remaining navies in the Central American/Caribbean region, only that of Nicaragua's beleaguered Sandinista Revolutionary Government has any combat potential. This takes the form of a small number of North Korean Sin Hung-class torpedo attack craft.

Ex-USN *Cannon*-class frigate *Uruguay* of the Uruguayan Navy.

Minor Latin American navies

Of the minor Latin American navies, only those of Uruguay and, surprisingly, land-locked Paraguay merit serious attention.

The Uruguayan Navy is a small coastal patrol force based on three elderly ex-US destroyer escorts, an Auk-class minesweeper converted into a corvette, three recently completed French-built patrol vessels, and about half a dozen small patrol craft, most of which are operated by the paramilitary *Prefectura Naval* coastguard. There is no effective sealift or amphibious assault capability for the country's single marine battalion. The naval air arm does however have an adequate patrol and ASW force in the form of six Grumman Trackers and a single Beech Super King Air, and a light strike capability comprising nine armed North American T-28 trainers.

The Paraguayan Navy – whose operations are confined to the Paraguay and Paraná rivers, both more than 1,000 miles from the nearest salt water – consists of two 55-year-old armoured gunboats, a recently completed helicopter-capable river patrol vessel of the Brazilian *Roraíma* type, three ex-Argentinian minesweepers employed as corvettes, a Second World War-vintage US-built LSM converted for minelaying and with helicopter-handling capability, and half a dozen small patrol launches. Paraguay also has a small marine corps and a naval air arm which is mainly a transport and helicopter force.

Latin America's other totally landlocked country, Bolivia, has a small naval force consisting of motor launches operating on its navigable lake and river system, a maritime battalion and a few light aircraft.

Summary and prospects

Of the major Latin American navies, both Argentina and Brazil will need to replace their aircraft carriers in the near future. The supply of second-hand carriers is now limited to the point of non-existence, although either *Clemenceau* or *Foch*, if not both, can be expected to find their way into the hands of the South American big four when they are disposed of by the French Navy in the mid-1990s. The most likely immediate solution to the problem of the replacement of the *Veinticinco de Mayo* and the *Minas Gerais* would however seem to lie in the local construction of either a version of the US Sea Control Ship or of a carrier based on a commercial hull. But both of these are unsatisfactory in being designed primarily to operate V/STOL aircraft, which for both economic and political reasons seem destined to remain beyond the

reach of all Latin American navies for the foreseeable future.

The Chilean Navy – and presumably also that of Peru – is almost desperate to acquire embarked naval combat aviation, the Chileans having been disappointed by the refusal of the British Government to sell them HMS *Hermes*. A possible solution to their problem would seem to be the conversion of at least one of their existing cruiser hulls, and the Chilean Navy has already carried out studies of the conversion of the *O'Higgins* into a carrier of either fixed-wing aircraft or helicopters. The Chileans would also like to acquire two more modern submarines and up to four additional *Leander*-class frigates, and have plans for the construction of up to six *Reshef*-class missile boats in their own yards. The Peruvians, for their part, can be expected to rearm their eight old Dutch destroyers with SSMs and will not scruple to turn to the Soviets for this equipment if Western manufacturers prove unwilling.

The remaining craft in Argentina's submarine construction programme can be expected to materialise in the medium term, and the Brazilians have stated that they will begin building nuclear-powered submarines during the 1990s. Both countries certainly possess the technology if not the economic resources to construct nuclear-powered naval vessels, and this must be taken seriously as a long-term development.

Of the smaller navies, that of Venezuela proposes to build at least two additional submarines and four corvettes in the medium term, and the Colombian Navy would like to build four missile corvettes, although official approval and hence funds both seem slow in coming. Colombia's infant naval air arm can also be expected to expand to include at least an adequate maritime patrol and ASW element. The Ecuadorians want at least one missile frigate, if only to serve as a command ship for the six *Esmeraldas*-class corvettes. Likely candidates include the Italian *Lupo* and Spanish *Descubierta* designs.

The Mexican Navy has embarked on a modest programme of construction in local yards of additional EEZ patrol vessels and smaller patrol craft. But the acquisition of a force of Swedish *Spica*-class fast attack craft, rumoured in the mid-1970s, now seems remote. The Uruguayan Navy's chances of getting two Type 209 submarines seem equally slim, although its air arm may acquire additional maritime patrol aircraft.

Above right: **The French attack carrier *Foch* is likely to find her way into South American hands some time in the 1990s. (*Giorgio Arra*)**

Right: **Chile is planning to build six missile boats to the Israeli *Reshef* design. (*A. D. Baker III*)**

The Dominican Navy seems to have little prospect of receiving new material, and its continued viability as a naval force must soon become problematic.

The Cuban Navy looks destined to continue to grow, probably acquiring at least one submarine and a frigate annually until a force of at least six vessels of each type is built up. Likewise, continued hostile pressures from the United States will probably prompt the development of the Nicaraguan Navy into at least a viable coast defence force with up to a dozen missile and torpedo attack craft. The likelihood of the acquisition of major seagoing vessels remains remote, however.

US attempts to expand both the Salvadorean and Honduran navies have resulted in an increase in the offshore patrol capabilities of each, while a force of marine commandos have been formed in El Salvador with US assistance. Spectacular expansion of the other

Ecuador is seeking a missile frigate for use as command ship with her squadron of *Esmeraldas*-class corvettes. The Italian *Lupo* and (illustrated here) Spanish *Descubiertas* are the favourites.

Central American and Caribbean navies seems unlikely, with the notable exception of that of Panama. The Panamanians must acquire some combat capability, probably in the form of a small force of missile attack craft and possibly also a mine warfare component, as the date for the assumption of full responsibility for the defence of the Panama Canal approaches.

Latin American naval development currently seems unusually static. An improvement in the economic situation, or an increase in regional tensions, could well result in a dramatic change to this state of affairs.

South-east Asia: a key alliance under pressure

Capt John Moore RN

The validity of the precept "divide and rule" is clearly demonstrated by the history of the last two or three thousand years. On the comparatively rare occasions when an alliance has remained cohesive, the outcome of its economic, political or military actions has generally been successful. In the last 40 years NATO has provided an excellent example of such a success, while other groupings like the Baghdad Pact (CENTO) and the South East Asia Treaty Organisation (SEATO) have been dissolved. The results could have been predicted: a sort of peace has been maintained in Europe and North America, while the Gulf and South-east Asia are in an unstable and dangerous condition.

When NATO was founded in 1947 the European countries were floundering in the wake of six years of disaster and destruction. The dismemberment of the colonial empires began in the same year, leading within two decades to the fragmentation of large areas into a multitude of small states. Although these nations had achieved the primary goal of political independence, their economies were fragile and, in many cases, their methods of government open to criticism from the democracies. Two problems contributed to this situation: the transition to self-help had in many cases been too abrupt, and the natural inclination was often towards the "chief and Indians" solution rather than the complexities of elected government. This turbulent situation was not helped by the fact that the two strongest countries in the world, the USA and USSR, had been pitchforked into a position of global leadership for which neither had any experience.

The USSR had the advantage of continuity of policy. Since the foundation of Comintern in 1920, the spread of subversion, with the ultimate aim of Soviet domination, had been continuous. The post-war disintegration of the European empires provided an excellent opportunity for a more active policy. Contained in Europe and frustrated in Iran and Korea, the Soviets expanded their more clandestine operations worldwide and found several lodgements in South-east Asia.

The policymakers of the USA, having launched the greatest display of generosity in history, the Marshall Plan, could see satisfactory results of their beneficence in the recovery of Europe. But elsewhere their touch was less sure. Following the McCarthy-inspired removal of the small number of people with experience of Chinese affairs, the spectre of communism in South-east Asia was allowed to sway the judgement of those in charge. China was of far less importance as an exporter of villainy than her Soviet neighbour, with whom relations had reached a low point in 1960. The entanglement in Vietnam, followed by the US withdrawal in 1972 and the enunciation of the Nixon Doctrine, changed the whole situation. Thenceforward direct involvement was renounced, though the US was to aid those prepared to help themselves. This laid an increased burden on the naval and air forces of the USA, the former having suffered markedly, if indirectly, from the diversion of funds to the war in Vietnam at a time when new construction was urgently needed.

In 1977 the new constitution of the USSR contained a commitment to assist "wars of national liberation," so formalising a practice pursued over the previous 60 years. The late 1970s were also notable for the steady decline of the policy of détente between the superpowers. Soviet support for the invasion of Cambodia by Vietnam alarmed both China and the USA. In 1979 one of the pillars of America's Middle Eastern policy was demolished by the Iranian revolution, which was followed in December of that year by the Soviet invasion of Afghanistan.

The Americans' reaction to what seemed to be a serious threat to US interests was to increase their naval presence in the Indian Ocean. The Rapid Deployment Force was formed and based at Diego Garcia, the use of which by US forces had first been discussed with the British in 1963. Elements of the US 6th Fleet in the Mediterranean and the 7th Fleet in the Pacific were deployed to the area. But, even in these days of highly sophisticated afloat support, there are certain things that can only be done by specialised services at a shore base. Such facilities are unavailable at Diego Garcia, and the nearest centre for the US fleet is at Subic Bay in the Philippines.

Subic Bay and the US Air Force base at Clark Field,

Left: **The Royal Thai Navy operates a trio of Italian-built fast attack craft armed with four Exocets each. This is *Ratcharit*, first of class.**

Above: **US Navy carrier battle group operating in the Indian Ocean (top), and a Soviet task force centred on a *Moskva*-class helicopter carrier (above). While the Russians enjoy secure bases in Vietnam, the Americans can only feel continuing unease about their lodgement in the Philippines (*US Navy*)**

are held under an agreement valid until 1991. But the reaction against the works of ex-president Marcos may see an end to this accord long before then. If this were to happen the search for an alternative would be difficult and the effects on the US Navy's deployment significant. There is a minor base at Guam, 1,500 miles to the east, but this is too distant; even if it were not, its conversion for fleet use would be extremely costly. The other ASEAN countries – Thailand, Malaysia, Indonesia and Singapore – might well balk at the measure of commitment implied by the granting of base rights. The attitude of Australia is equivocal to say the least, and New Zealand is too far distant in both miles and opinions. The future of the Philippines is therefore a matter of considerable moment for the USA and, rather less directly, for the USSR. The Soviet Navy is currently emplaced across the South China Sea at Da Nang and Cam Ranh Bay, the well equipped bases which the Americans quit when they left Vietnam. A slow but steady reinforcement of the Vietnamese Navy and a regular flow of logistic support form the payment for Soviet use of these facilities, which is of concern not only to the surrounding countries of ASEAN but also to the Chinese, watching from the northern border of Vietnam. This is barely 800 miles from Cam Ranh Bay and, were the Chinese so minded, a determined advance by their forces could place Soviet tenure at risk. Chinese submarines operating from Hai Nan would add a second dimension to such an operation. Certainly, Beijing is little pleased by the appearance of a Soviet fleet well based in a warm-water port beyond the Soviet Union's southern extremity and within easy reach of zones of possible dispute such as the Spratly and Paracel Islands.

TNC 45-class missile-armed fast attack craft of the Republic of Singapore Navy. Armament comprises five Gabriel anti-ship missiles, a 57mm Bofors gun and a 40mm cannon. (*L. & L. van Ginderen*)

Other problems arise from the perennial threat of piracy along the coasts of the South China Sea. Working in small, fast craft, the pirates who operate in the southern exits of the Malacca Strait frequently board large vessels under way in these narrow and congested waters. In recent years such attacks have occurred with increasing frequency, causing the Singapore authorities to integrate the activities of their various maritime forces. Indonesia has fewer resources and a problem compounded by a second area of piratical activity in the Sulu Sea between North-east Borneo and the Philippines. Here the attacks are more frequent and directed at smaller vessels, resulting in a higher death roll. The Filipino Navy has little strength to spare to combat these ferocious and well armed gangs. The same is true of the Thai Navy, which has a depressingly huge task in the Gulf of Siam. In this region, where pirate craft can lurk amongst the tens of thousands of fishing boats, the chief targets are still the Vietnamese boat people, of whom something like three-quarters have suffered theft, rape and death in their search for freedom. The pirates may be either Thais or Vietnamese, and their activities have stretched the small anti-piracy unit of the Thai Navy to the limit.

This fleet and that of Malaysia are expanding steadily. The Thais are building ships of corvette size and below, while the Malaysians, with extensive coastal areas to the east and west of the Malay

The plague of piracy in the South China Sea stretches the resources of the Royal Thai Navy to the limits. Typical of the craft used for this task is the *Swift*-class patrol boat, acquired from the US Navy nearly 20 years ago.

Peninsula as well as in North Borneo, have recently acquired two modern frigates and three much needed logistic support ships. The latter three ships are unusually versatile, having facilities for command and control, support of light forces and MCM vessels, and troop carrying. Their main deficiency appears to be the lack of an on-board helicopter, though a landing deck is provided. Ships of this type would be a sensible investment for navies in South-east Asia, increasing

Sri Indera Sakti, one of Malaysia's three versatile logistic support ships. Facilities include a helicopter deck, vehicle deck, port and starboard embarkation ramps, operations and conference rooms, and a recompression chamber. (*Bremer Vulkan*)

the flexibility of smaller vessels in an area notable for long passage distances. The fact that Sri Lanka has found it necessary to convert six merchant ships for this purpose to cover a comparatively small zone of conflict is indicative of the value of such support.

The island of Singapore has a strategic and financial importance far transcending its physical size. The authorities there have overcome many problems over the last 20 years, and the current crop of difficulties should prove equally surmountable. With a busy and vibrant population under determined and imaginative leadership, the island lies at the confluence of several ocean trading routes, with some 200 merchant ships passing every day. The Malacca Strait, though narrow and shallow in places, is the best route for naval vessels entering or leaving the Indian Ocean. Singapore's small but effective navy, with a number of fast missile craft, could seriously impede such reinforcement were the island's interests at risk.

The Indonesian Navy is faced with a task of daunting proportions. The country's population of some 160 million is spread over an ocean area of over seven million square miles, lives on over 3,000 islands and has one of the lowest per capita incomes in the world. While Indonesia's physical extent demands a large fleet for even the most minimal of surveillance, want of finance limits the programme to well below the numbers needed. Nevertheless, the planned

Malahayati, second of Indonesia's *Fatahillah*-class frigates.

strength of four frigates, six submarines, a sizeable force of patrol and missile craft, mine warfare vessels, a headquarters ship and a fast supply ship will meet a proportion of the requirement. The subsequent addition of helicopter-capable ships similar to the Malaysian logistic support vessels would make operational and financial sense.

Indonesia's position in Australian defence planning is only one of many problems exercising the strategies of Canberra. Their task is made no easier by an internal diversity of opinions, ranging from attitudes

HMAS *Canberra*, one of the four FFG-7-class frigates operated by the Royal Australian Navy. (*Ron Wright*)

which can give no comfort to anybody outside the Soviet Union to a more sober focus on "the defence of Australia and its interests". But defence against what and whom? The geographical situation of this vast, empty land, which encompasses every form of climate short of the polar excesses, sets defence planners a multitude of problems even more intractable than those facing their European colleagues. The great archipelago to the north would be an obvious source of danger should it be overrun by hostile powers. From Sumatra in the west, through New Guinea to Tuvalu and Tokelau in the east, a huge expanse of islands could provide lodgement for an enemy power with designs on the countries further south. Already the Soviet Union has approached the Solomons and Tuvalu for fishing rights, the traditional first step of infiltration into less developed countries. Though these overtures have been unsuccessful so far, the leaders of Kiribati to the north have struck a deal, opening to Soviet surveillance some 30% of the ocean south of the Equator for an annual fee of less than £750,000. Vanuatu, an arc of islands nearly 1,000 miles long and the same distance from the Queensland coast, is considering a similar agreement. The Australians are in danger of being outflanked in the same way as the Americans in the Caribbean. Diplomatic moves to win over the Pacific island nations are therefore a matter of urgency.

Australia's involvement in the Vietnam War was probably the last time that her forces would be landed on mainland Asia. They made their passage under American protection and were gratefully received, and few reflected on the significance of this situation. But is American protection still available to Australia at a time when the US Navy is stretched to provide adequate forces in the northern Pacific and the Indian Ocean? Australia has a number of significant maritime interests: shipping routes for 99% of her trade and

their protection in the Indian Ocean and South China Sea, free access to her ports, and the safety of her fishing and offshore industries. Any disruption of any of these would have an immediate effect on the nation. And if hostilities of any type were to develop in the archipelagoes, there would be an instant need for long-range surveillance and operations in those areas.

The huge distances involved would put a high premium on air operations, for which the Royal Australian Navy, without any carrierborne fixed-wing aircraft, would have to rely on the air force. In-flight refuelling and airborne early warning are essential if such operations are to be successful. Another pressing requirement, given the formidable strength of the Soviet Pacific Fleet's submarine force, is a modern ASW capability. Eight ASW helicopters are on order, which means that about four would be operational at any one time. Many more are needed, as are ships to carry them. On the principle that the weapon systems are more important than the carriers, the use of converted merchant ships would be logical.

Britain's Royal Navy has pioneered this approach, having taken delivery of one such ship, *Reliant*, following an eight-month conversion to fit her to carry five Sea King helicopters. Another, *Argus*, is undergoing a more extensive rebuilding which will take two years at a cost of £30 million. The result will be a ship carrying six Sea Kings and with facilities for the operation of 12 Sea Harriers. The ship's complement of *Reliant* is 60, excluding the air group. This is almost exactly one eleventh of the figure for HMS *Invincible*, while the running cost – *Reliant* is powered by one 29,000bhp diesel – is correspondingly low.

The British solution to the problems of operations far from the support facilities of a main base: the forward repair ship HMS *Diligence*, formerly the North Sea support vessel *Stena Inspector*. (*Crown Copyright*)

Three other RN conversions are also relevant in the context of long-range operations with little base support. The first is the 10,595-ton HMS *Diligence*, formerly an oil rig support vessel and now a forward repair ship in the Falkland Islands, where two of her charges are HMS *Guardian* and *Protector*. These sturdy oil rig supply vessels have been converted as patrol ships but are equally suitable for hydrographic and other duties. Such inexpensive solutions could be of great value to the Royal Australian Navy, whose numbers and budget are both inadequate for a multiplicity of tasks on a very lengthy coastline.

Meanwhile, the total force, apart from coastal and support ships and craft, is six submarines, three destroyers, nine frigates and an amphibious ship.

These figures make it clear that in a crisis co-operation with other navies would be essential. This was foreseen in the ANZUS agreement of 1951, which has subsequently benefitted all three participants. The Prime Minister of Australia remains firmly in favour of the agreement and has recently done a great deal to uphold it. His efforts have been made necessary by the New Zealand Government's decision to ban foreign naval ships with nuclear propulsion or weapons from its territorial waters. This has effectively put at risk the whole structure of ANZUS and deprived New Zealand of several types of military support, most notably the intelligence input from the USA. Such are the limited capabilities of the New Zealand intelligence services, the government is now unlikely to be aware of the presence of Soviet nuclear-propelled submarines in its waters.

This development can only give comfort to Soviet planners, since it not only denies the US Navy valuable base facilities in an area of crucial importance but has also shaken the cohesion of the only pro-Western alliance in the region. Thriving as divisions between nations, infiltration and disinformation become far less effective if faced on a broad front by groups of countries whose interests are generally similar. "Divide and rule" currently has more significance for the Kremlin in the South-west Pacific than it has almost anywhere else in the rest of the world.

HMNZS *Canterbury*, one of New Zealand's quartet of British-built *Leander*-class frigates. (*Graeme K. Andrews Productions*)

US Ready Reserve Force: lifeboats for a nation

Nigel Ling

The oiler (AO) *American Explorer*, now laid up at Beaumont, Texas. (*L. & L. van Ginderen*)

In parallel with the decline of most of the Western nations' merchant fleets, the numbers of ships in the US Merchant Marine that could be requisitioned in emergency has dwindled alarmingly. Awareness of this deficiency resulted in an agreement between the Navy and Transportation departments in October 1982 to set up the Ready Reserve Force (RRF), a fleet of merchant ships of specific types to be laid up in a state of five or ten days' readiness at three bases in the United States. The Maritime Administration (MARAD) was given the job of acquiring, laying up and maintaining these vessels.

By the end of the first, 1983–85, stage of the programme 59 ships, comprising 51 cargo vessels, seven tankers and one crane ship, had been acquired and laid up. The majority were divided between the James River, Virginia; Beaumont, Texas; and Suisun Bay, California. These locations, at three of the nation's four corners, were chosen to minimise the time of response to contingencies in the North Atlantic, Caribbean and Pacific respectively.

Development of the RRF continues. MARAD requested $203.4 million for Fiscal Year 1986 for further expansion, and a request for proposals was circulated to shipowners in March 1985, specifying the types and characteristics of the vessels required. The numbers of ships ultimately acquired will depend on the prices at which they are offered, although it is hoped that the RRF will have expanded to a total of 116 ships by 1991.

The FY86 budget covers vessels for delivery before September 30, 1986, and in March 1985 MARAD held a conference to explain the request for proposals in detail to shipowners. Seven required ship types have been identified and ranked in order of military utility. It is no coincidence that they are exactly those that the Soviet Union has concentrated on in recent years to upgrade the specialist tonnage of its merchant fleet. In only two of the seven categories – Ro-Ro and heavy-lift ships – may a vessel be of non-US construction. This requirement may prove to be unnecessarily

Cargo ship (AK) *Southern Cross* in her original civilian guise as *Mormactrade*.

The review and selection procedure for the FY86 ships, including surveying and performance trials, was expected to last seven months. After selection, owners would be given the opportunity to maintain and operate the ships as part of the RRF. Principal criteria in the evaluation and selection of individual ships are price and military utility. Price ceiling is based on a defined maximum cost per unit of load-carrying capacity. Military utility is a function of factors such as additional cargo space above the specified minimum, cargo-handling gear, range, speed, damage-resistance, manoeuvrability, and ballasting and propulsion characteristics. Finally, each ship must be able to pass through the Suez and Panama canals.

Roll-on/Roll-off ships

There are four Ro-Ro ships under US flag, and suitable tonnage is also likely to be offered from many other parts of the world. Main specific requirement is an installed stern or quarter ramp with a capacity of at least 65 tons, a minimum overhead clearance of 14ft and a width of 17ft. The ramp angle should not exceed 15°. Ro-Ro space must be at least 100,000ft^2, of which 70,000ft^2 must be below deck and 30,000ft^2 stiffened to accept an imposed load of 525lb/ft^2; minimum headroom is 13ft. A loaded service speed of 17kt is required.

restrictive, as there are many surplus foreign-built, foreign-flag vessels in which US owners or finance companies have interests, and it is likely to be relaxed in the future.

MARAD has no intention of being palmed off with owners' "lame ducks" and has laid down stringent but fair requirements. No ship built before 1965 will be considered. Vessels acquired must be delivered with five days' fuel and lubricants remaining, fully certificated for all US requirements, drydocked, surveyed, painted grey and fully operational, the last defined as "capable of steaming continuously in unrestricted operation for at least 180 days".

Vehicle cargo ship (AKR) *Comet* has a built-in roll-on/roll-off ramp system. (*L. & L. van Ginderen*)

Heavy-lift ships

There are currently no heavy-lift ships in the RRF, and they will almost certainly have to be bought from abroad. While the specified 210-ton lift capacity is useful for handling a wide range of military equipment, the heavy-lift ships are specifically required to carry four LCUs of the 1466 or 1667 type at a 12kt service speed.

Barge-carrying ships

The Soviet Union is building barge-carriers in increasing numbers, not only for their valuable ability to transport cargoes to areas with few or no port facilities, but also for their usefulness in the assault role. Though such ships are of high military value, their numbers are unlikely to increase significantly in the West on account of their high capital costs and the want of routes on which they can be operated economically.

Requirements include a 17kt loaded service speed and a full set of barges and containers.

Clean-products tankers

In past conflicts there have never been enough tankers to meet the demand for petroleum products. In 1982 a total of 15 tankers were taken up from trade by the British to augment the ten RFA tankers used in the Falklands War. Over a year later nine civilian tankers were still fully engaged in the support of a relatively modest garrison and development effort. This gives some indication of the large numbers of vessels that would be required to support a major US overseas operation.

A service speed of 13.5kt is specified, with deadweight to be between 20,000 tons and the Panama Canal limit. The ability to carry two different grades of cargo is required, together with tank coatings compatible with the carriage of jet fuels.

Potomac, **assigned to the Ready Reserve Force and laid up at Suisun Bay, has a chequered history. Built from the stern of a naval tanker destroyed by fire, plus new forward sections, she was originally named** *Shenandoah*.

While there are many suitable tankers on the market, the requirement for US construction will limit the number of vessels offered and may prove to be impossibly restrictive.

Cargo ship *Pride* is one of three RRF vessels laid up at Philadelphia Naval Shipyard. (*Giorgio Arra*)

Self-sustaining breakbulk ships

The self-sustaining general cargo ship has been the workhorse of merchant fleets around the world for the past 100 years. Following the increase in use of container ships, gearless bulk carriers and other specialised tonnage, the number of traditional cargo vessels in the Western fleets has diminished. Many of the more modern types require extensive investment in shore facilities, and would be of limited value in any operation in undeveloped areas or where port facilities had been destroyed.

The requirement is for 400,000ft³ capacity, 17kt ships having all holds served both sides by cranes or derricks with a minimum capacity of five tons, and a 65-ton jumbo derrick serving at least one hold. Such ships are readily available and the acquisition of suitable examples should be relatively straightforward.

Container ships for conversion into auxiliary crane ships

Modern container ships are mostly gearless and rely totally on shore-based equipment for loading and discharge of cargo. Container cranes are expensive and found only in major ports, and their location and construction make them vulnerable to air attack and sabotage. Such facilities are more vulnerable than the ships they are designed to serve, and it is quite possible that in war a container ship could make a successful passage only to find the necessary cargo-handling equipment destroyed.

With this in mind, general cargo and container ships are being acquired and converted into auxiliary crane ships (T-ACS). Such vessels would also be of great use in amphibious operations and in handling exceptionally large items of military equipment. Ships dimensions must exceed 500ft × 73ft × 40ft, with a service speed of 17kt.

The prototype T-ACS *Keystone State*, was approved under the FY82 programme. Conversion began in March 1983 and was completed in June 1984. Conversion of her sister ship *Gem State* is approaching completion, and further suitable hulls are being sought. Principal additional equipment comprises three twin-boom pedestal cranes with jibs long enough to discharge onto the quayside a container ship lying between the T-ACS and the quay. Conversion cost is about $40 million per vessel.

LASH barges

Spare sets of LASH (lighter-aboard-ship) barges are needed to keep the barge-carriers fully employed. For any barge-carrier operating between two fixed ports, three complete outfits of barges are required to minimise downtime: one set at sea and one set being worked in each port. About 200 barges per ship will therefore be required. The facilities to series-produce barges in these numbers are available in the Soviet Union, where the military utility of the LASH system has long been recognised.

Deactivation and future use

After acceptance survey and purchase – together with any modifications and upgrading of the communications equipment, which includes the provision of the Marisat satellite communications system – the vessels are moved to one of the three lay-up areas. While strategic considerations dictate most locations, draught is sometimes a constraint, with Beaumont being limited to 16ft, Suisun Bay to 18ft, and James River to 24ft.

The ships are maintained at five or ten days' notice for sea. Regular exercises are to be carried out to test resupply and voyage procedures, and "no notice" reactivations will be ordered to ensure that the vessels can be ready for sea in the prescribed time. All spares and equipment for 180 days' continuous steaming are maintained on board, together with operating instructions and procedures, so that any group of competent officers and men can board any ship in the RRF and take her to sea without further training.

Little deactivation work is done on short-notice ships other than the draining down of tanks and fluids, normal anti-corrosive treatments, blanking-off of discharges, and the fitting of blanks to seachests in such a way that they can be readily removed by divers. Ships on longer notice are sealed and dehumidified, with all external openings made airtight.

The existence of the RRF allows supporting operations to be conducted without disruption to normal trading patterns as a result of the requisitioning of active merchant ships. It also shows an awareness of the value of reliable sealift, with ships of known quality and characteristics, and of the fact that the success of any overseas operation can only be assured if the supply of stores, fuel and equipment can be guaranteed.

The British merchant fleet has now shrunk to a level at which it would be almost impossible to sustain another Falklands-style operation. While no equivalent of the Ready Reserve Force can be envisaged, it is high time that steps were taken to prevent its further decline. But apart from one short paragraph in the 1985 Defence White Paper promising a "major study," there is little to suggest that anything will be done in the near future. It is therefore encouraging to see that our major ally is aware that the projection of sea power is ultimately dependent on more mundane factors than the numbers of front-line ships and aircraft available.

The petrol tanker *Chattahoochee* pictured while on Military Sealift Command service in Antarctica. (*US Navy*)

US Ready Reserve Force*

Name/Type	Hull design	Days notice	Current status
Pride (AK)	C3-S-33a	10	Reserve: Philadelphia Naval Shipyard
Scan (AK)	C3-S-33a	5	Reserve: Philadelphia Naval Shipyard
Lake (AK)	C3-S-33a	10	Reserve: Philadelphia Naval Shipyard
Adventurer (AK)	C3-S-38a	10	Reserve: MARAD, James River
Agent (AK)	C3-S-38a	10	Reserve: Cheatham Naval Annex
Aide (AK)	C3-S-38a	10	Reserve: MARAD, James River
Ambassador (AK)	C3-S-38a	10	Reserve: MARAD, James River
Banner (AK)	C3-S-46a	10	Reserve: MARAD, James River
Courier (AK)	C3-S-46b	10	Reserve: MARAD, James River
Cracker State Mariner (AK)	C4-S-1h	10	Reserve: MARAD, James River
President (AK)	C4-S-1qb	5	Reserve: MARAD, Suisun Bay
Lincoln (AK)	C4-S-1qb	5	Reserve: MARAD, Suisun Bay
Santa Ana (AK)	C4-S-1u	10	Reserve: MARAD, Beaumont
California (AK)	C4-S-1u	5	Reserve: MARAD, Suisun Bay
Pioneer Commander (AK)	C4-S-57a	10	Reserve: MARAD, Beaumont
Pioneer Contractor (AK)	C4-S-57a	10	Reserve: MARAD, Beaumont
Pioneer Crusader (AK)	C4-S-57a	10	Reserve: MARAD, Beaumont
Cape Alava (AK)	C4-S-58a	10	Reserve: MARAD, James River
Cape Ann (AK)	C4-S-58a	10	Reserve: MARAD, James River
Cape Alexander (AK)	C4-S-58a	10	Reserve: MARAD, James River
Cape Archway (AK)	C4-S-58a	10	Reserve: MARAD, James River
Cape Avinof (AK)	C4-S-58a	10	Reserve: MARAD, James River
Catawba Victory (AK)	VC2-S-AP12	10	Reserve: MARAD, James River
Maine (AK)	Seatrain	10	Reserve: MARAD, Beaumont
Washington (AK)	Seatrain	10	Reserve: MARAD, Beaumont
Ohio (AK)	Seatrain	10	Reserve: MARAD, James River
Chancellorsville (AOT)	T2-SE-A1j	10	Reserve: MARAD, Beaumont
Keystone State (ACS)	T-ACS1/CG-S-1qd	5	Reserve: Cheatham Annex
Great Republic (AKR)	C5-S-78a	5	Reserve: MARAD, James River
Santa Barbara (AK)	C4-S-65	5	Reserve: MARAD, James River
Santa Clara (AK)	C4-S-65	5	Reserve: MARAD, James River
Santa Cruz (AK)	C4-S-65	5	Reserve: MARAD, James River
Santa Elena (AK)	C4-S-65	5	Reserve: MARAD, James River
Santa Isabel (AK)	C4-S-65	5	Reserve: MARAD, James River
Santa Lucia (AK)	C4-S-65	10	Reserve: MARAD, James River
Aimee Lykes (AK)	C3-S-37	10	Reserve: MARAD, James River
Allison Lykes (AK)	C3-S-37	10	Reserve: MARAD, James River
Margaret Lykes (AK)	C3-S-37	10	Reserve: MARAD, James River
Christopher Lykes (AK)	C3-S-37	10	Reserve: MARAD, James River
Southen Cross (AK)	C3-S-33	5	Reserve: MARAD, James River
Del Viento (AK)	C3-S-76a	5	Reserve: MARAD, Beaumont
Adabelle Lykes (AK)	C3-S-37	10	Reserve: MARAD, Beaumont
Charlotte Lykes (AK)	C3-S-37	10	Reserve: MARAD, Beaumont
Mayo Lykes (AK)	C3-S-37	10	Reserve: MARAD, Beaumont
Sheldon Lykes (AK)	C3-S-37	10	Reserve: MARAD, Beaumont
Gulf Banker (AK)	C3-S-37	10	Reserve: MARAD, Beaumont
Gulf Farmer (AK)	C3-S-37	10	Reserve: MARAD, Beaumont
Gulf Trader (AK)	C3-S-37	10	Reserve: MARAD, Beaumont
Gulf Shipper (AK)	C3-S-37	10	Reserve: MARAD, Beaumont
Gulf Merchant (AK)	C3-S-37	10	Reserve: MARAD, Beaumont
Del Valle (AK)	C3-S-76a	10	Reserve: MARAD, Beaumont
Del Monte (AK)	C3-S-76a	10	Reserve: MARAD, Beaumont
ex-USNS *American Explorer* (AO)	T-5	10	Reserve: MARAD, Beaumont
ex-USNS *Potomac* (AO)	T-5	10	Reserve: MARAD, Suisun Bay
ex-USNS *Nodaway* (AOE)	T1-B2	10	Reserve: Pearl Harbor
ex-USNS *Chattahoochee* (AOG)	T1-ME	10	Reserve: Japan
ex-USNS *Alatna* (AOG)	T1-ME	10	Reserve: Japan
ex-USNS *Northern Light* (AK)	C3-S-33a	10	Reserve: MARAD, Suisun Bay
ex-USNS *Shoshone* (AO)	T-5	10	Reserve: MARAD, Suisun Bay
ex-USNS *Comet* (AKR)	C3-ST-14a	?	Reserve: MARAD, Suisun Bay
Austral Lightning (LASH)	?	?	Reserve: MARAD, Suisun Bay
Frederick Lykes (AK)	?	?	Reserve: MARAD, Suisun Bay

* As of April 1, 1985.

Cargo ship *Northern Light*, sister ship to *Southern Cross* and formerly known as *Mormaccove*.

The petrol tanker (AOG) *Alatna*, one of two RRF ships positioned in Japan. (*L. & L. van Ginderen*)

Who shall defend the Canadian Arctic?

John D. Harbron

Artist's impression of Canada's Polar 8, which will be the world's largest icebreaker – 35,000 tons deadweight and 100,000shp – when she enters service in 1989–90. (*Canadian Coast Guard*)

The Canadian Government's announcement last year that a start was finally made on building the long-overdue Polar 8 large icebreaker to extend Arctic sovereignty protection did nothing to settle the questions surrounding future naval defence policy for this region. Despite the fact that in the giant Polar 8, at 35,000 tons deadweight and 100,000 shaft horse-power, Canada will have the world's largest icebreaker and the first in history to operate year-round in the nation's Arctic waters, the decision on who should own her – navy or coastguard – is left up in the air.

The confusion began on September 10 when External Affairs Minister Joe Clark announced a go-ahead for Polar 8, design of which was finished in 1982, without indicating who would operate her. He went on to promise "immediate planning for Canadian naval activity in the Eastern Arctic in 1986." But none of Canada's warships – the 22 ageing destroyers and three conventional submarines now in service, and the new Canadian Patrol Frigates (CPFs), construction of

which has just begun – has icebreaking capability. With the sole exception of HMCS *Labrador* – Canada's one and only naval icebreaker, which served in the old Royal Canadian Navy between 1954 and 1958 – this major Arctic power has never built a naval vessel that can operate in ice.

The present configuration of Polar 8, so designated in recognition of its planned ability to do a continuous eight knots through eight feet of ice, includes no underwater detection capability such as strategic or tactical towed array sonar (SURTAS/TACTAS) for submarine surveillance. Nor will the big ship function in the same way as the Soviet icebreakers that are close

151

to her in size. These include the two 75,000shp nuclear-powered *Sibir*-class icebreakers and *Tamyr*, the 52,000shp nuclear vessel at present under construction at the Helsinki shipyard of Finnish company Wärtsilä. Polar 8 will operate alone in such civilian roles as oceanographic research and enforcement of Canada's tough Arctic environmental protection regulations, as well as on sovereignty surveillance missions. The big Soviet nuclear icebreakers, by comparison, are part of an integrated icebreaking operation serving the many commercial ports at the Siberian river estuaries along the Arctic coast. Canada's underdeveloped Arctic has no ports the size of those along the USSR's Northern Sea Route, and such empty regions simplify the task of foreign submarines operating secretly in Canadian Arctic waters.

Given Polar 8's many non-naval roles, it is easy to understand why the admirals in command of Canada's

Left: **HMCS *Labrador*, which served with the Royal Canadian Navy in 1954–58, is the only ice-capable vessel ever to have been built for the Canadian naval forces.**

Below: **The 9,120-ton *John A. Macdonald* is currently Canada's largest icebreaker.**

The very large and capable Soviet icebreaking fleet is tasked with maintaining access to Western Arctic ports for both Russian and foreign shipping. More exceptionally, ships like the nuclear-powered *Sibir* (left) and diesel-engined *Kapitan Sorokin* have also proved successful at extricating vessels trapped in the ice. (*Tass*)

The shallow-draught nuclear icebreaker *Tamyr*, designed for operation in Soviet Arctic river estuaries. At 52,000shp she will have half the installed power of Canada's Polar 8. (*Wartsila*)

minuscule navy, which needs all the new ships it can get, are reported not to want the new icebreaker. They insist that Canada's present naval manpower cannot be stretched in the 1990s to man and service both the giant Polar 8 and the six new CPFs. The latter are being built to maintain the Canadian Navy's historic and important contribution to NATO as one of the most experienced anti-submarine warfare fleets in the North Atlantic. The first CPF is due to commission at the same time as Polar 8, in late 1989 or early 1990.

The admirals' other objections are technical in nature. Polar 8 could not easily be reconfigured as a naval icebreaker, given her hull design and the fact that her mission profile already includes 12 civilian tasks. Further, a key naval system, towed-array sonar, does not work well in icebreakers, whether for submarine surveillance or ice profiling for scientific research. The grinding from ice movements and the loud noise of icebreaker engines render sonar findings almost useless. Polar 8's design team has already rejected the use of towed-array sonar for non-naval oceanographic studies.

If Polar 8 cannot do the job, what kind of ships should be in service to monitor the US surface ships and submarines, as well as Soviet and Royal Navy submarines, that operate in the region? The quandary is summed up by recently retired Rear Admiral Frederick Crickard, whose last naval appointment was Deputy Commander, Maritime Command: "If we are given the icebreaker [Polar 8] as a sop to the navy we will take it . . . because there is no well thought-out naval doctrine and there never has been. This failure has been part of the overall failure of the Department of National Defence at large to create one. An icebreaker with SURTAS represents a ship system not

Impression of the Canadian Patrol Frigate, six examples of which are due to enter service in the 1990s. (*Saint John Shipbuilding and Dry Dock Co*)

consistent with the naval force doctrine of Canada as a support to SACLANT. . . . Such a ship would very much be an odd man out. But if offered, we will do our best to make it into a warship."

There are thus no ships at present in service in Canada's navy or coastguard that could carry out the "naval activity" in the Eastern Arctic called for in the Clark statement. Many Canadian Arctic experts agree that the announcement was hastily contrived as a response to the Northwest Passage voyage in July 1985 of the United States Coast Guard icebreaker *Polar Sea*. Since the United States considers the Northwest Passage to be international and not Canadian territorial waters, no permission for the *Polar Sea*'s passage was requested. The voyage raised such public ire that the Canadian government was compelled to fall back on the Arctic Waters Shipping Pollution Prevention Act, which requires any ship in Arctic transit to certify that it is not an environmental hazard. *Polar Sea* was eventually granted permission under the Act, even though she has a record of being trapped in ice (for four months off Barrow, Alaska, between March and June, 1981) and had undergone propeller repairs in her Seattle home port before that event.

This highly controversial transit, which raised

US Coast Guard icebreaker *Polar Sea* stung the Canadian Government into a go-ahead on Polar 8 by transiting Canadian territorial waters in the Northwest Passage in July 1985. (*L. & L. van Ginderen*)

public indignation about Arctic sovereignty protection to a level not seen since the equally controversial voyages in 1969–1970 of the US icebreaker-tanker *Manhattan*, and the vexed question of Polar 8's ownership have brought the spotlight to bear on Canada's Arctic naval defences. But how great is the threat to Canadian sovereignty in the north compared with the obvious one from Soviet naval vessel and submarine movements off the country's east and west coasts. And if not with surface warships fitted for ice operations or a naval icebreaker, how else might Canada's Arctic interests be safeguarded?

there and would not try to operate in our Arctic waters.''

Another Arctic defence system under study is Radarsat, a Canadian-designed and built remote-

US postal cover mailed to commemorate the passage of the nuclear submarine USS *Hammerhead* beneath the North Pole in 1970. It also betrays an ignorance of – or indifference to? – the fact that Canada claims these waters as her own.

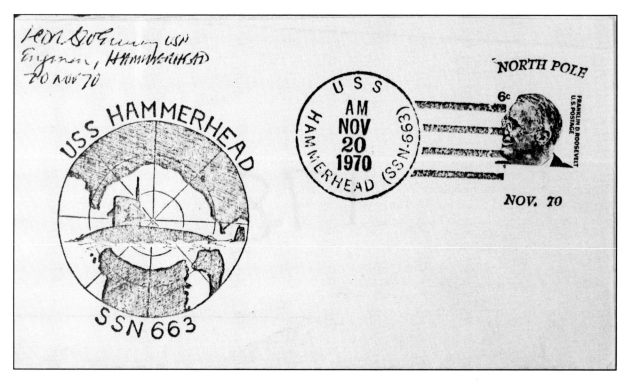

The possibility of buying two to four off-the-shelf nuclear submarines at a cost of between $2.5 and $4 billion, an option raised publicly in early 1984 at the end of the last Trudeau government, is still under consideration. A cheaper alternative could be a small fleet of conventionally powered submarines, which are quieter than nuclear boats and therefore better suited to the detection of the Soviet and US submarines that operate clandestinely in Canadian Arctic waters.

Less costly and much more likely to materialise are the networks of ocean-bottom sensors first proposed in the 1971 Defence White Paper. Covering the eastern sea entrances to the Canadian Arctic, they would require five years to install and cost an estimated $35 million. A more complex ocean-bottom sensor array could monitor the entire Arctic Basin, require a decade to build and cost about $45 million. Admiral Crickard is firmly in favour: "If we had them, . . . our own system on our own Arctic archipelago, then our friends and our potential enemy would know they are

sensing satellite that could locate and track all surface vessels in any kind of weather within a radius of 500 miles. This would cost about $360 million and probably be ready by 1991.

The trouble with all these programmes, vital though they are to Canada's control over her own Arctic waters, is that the government doesn't have the financial resources for any of them, least of all nuclear submarines.

The equipment problem is made worse by a matching lack of policy. The Canadian Government has no clear doctrine to cover sovereignty crises like the one provoked by *Polar Sea*'s transit, and is unlikely to define one in its long-delayed Defence White Paper, and the Department of National Defence repeatedly rejects outside professional advice. A 1983 brief from the Naval Officers' Association of Canada (NOAC) supporting a Canadian naval icebreaker and proposing some initial training of naval personnel on board the Coast Guard's icebreakers was ignored by

the navy. So was another NOAC brief reminding the Department of National Defence that Canada now had almost no minesweepers and no mine countermeasures (MCM) and that the country's vital seaports were therefore defenceless against possible Soviet mining.

The NOAC's 1983 brief reminded the navy that in the late 1950s the icebreaker HMCS *Labrador* became the first ship of its kind to traverse the Northwest Passage from east to west and return, a capability that will be restored by Polar 8 after an interval of three decades.

The debate over the ownership of Polar 8, which will cost half a billion dollars to build, has generated a new public awareness of Canada's appalling inability to assert itself as the world's second largest Arctic power after the Soviet Union. The indifference to national defence of the successive governments of former Prime Minister Pierre Trudeau (1968–1984) has had much to do with the nation's sad slide from

naval respectability in the mid-1960s to dismal inadequacy in the mid-1980s. But now the failure to define an Arctic naval defence doctrine has become a national issue, and it is to be hoped that the resulting public scrutiny will go some way towards repairing the damage.

Rising stakes in the Northern Waters

Clive Archer and David Scrivener

The UK-Iceland Cod War was the most bad-tempered conflict to break out in the Northern Waters since the end of the Second World War. Here the Icelandic gunboat *Baldur* makes a close run across the stern of the British trawler *Kingston Beryl*. (*Royal Navy*)

Until recently the waters to the north of the British Isles drew scant attention from politicians, writers or the public at large. Every so often, skirmishes between the United Kingdom and Iceland about fisheries limits attracted the media, but it was not until the mid-1970s that the importance of the Northern Waters was more widely recognised. Interest in their economic value was more sharply focused by the extension of economic and fisheries zones in 1977, and by the northwards move of oil and gas exploration. At the same time there was a marked increase in military activity in the area, due in no small part to its growing economic significance.[1]

The Northern Waters comprise the maritime areas within the latitudes 80°N and 60°N and the longitudes 90°W and 40°E. Land areas within these boundaries include the islands of Arctic Canada, Greenland, Iceland, the Faroes, the Shetlands, Jan Mayen, Svalbard and the Kola Peninsula. The region thus contains three important approaches: the Fram Straits between Greenland and Svalbard, leading from the

Polar Sea out to the Atlantic Ocean; the waters of the Baffin Bay-Davis Straits, joining the northern coasts of Alaska and Canada to the Atlantic Ocean and, in particular, the east coast of Canada and the USA; and the Barents and Norwegian seas, providing access into the Atlantic from the Arctic Ocean and the northern coasts of Norway and the Soviet Union. In addition to their political and economic significance, these passages are of great environmental interest. In this respect their high degree of vulnerability to pollutants is a matter for concern.[2]

The Northern Waters matter because of the areas they adjoin: they form the northern rim of the expanse crossed by the sea lanes between North America and Western Europe, and are the approaches to the Arctic Ocean, which itself has been typified as both a sea lying between the North Atlantic and the North Pacific, and a mediterranean sea bounded by the shores of North America and the northern stretches of Eurasia.[3] The interests of the two superpowers in the nearby territories are clear. While the extent of the riches of Siberia, Alaska and Northern Canada has only recently been appreciated, the strategic significance to the Soviet Union, America and the West at large of the Arctic lands has emerged over the past 35 years. This significance has waxed and waned as strategic bombers were supplemented by inter-

continental ballistic missiles (ICBMs), missile-launching submarines lurking in the Northern Waters, and long-range air-launched cruise missiles (ALCMs) and sea-launched cruise missiles (SLCMs).

As well as being an area of transit, the Northern Waters have an intrinsic value. In the past the

The introduction of new military technology into the region has increased the risk of superpower conflict in the Northern Waters. This US Navy A-6 Intruder has just launched a Boeing Air Launched Cruise Missile.

The natural riches of the region are a powerful attraction to the adjoining nations in spite of the formidable natural obstacles to exploitation. Many Soviet vessels combine economic functions with intelligence-gathering: this trawler is shadowing the US 2nd Fleet off Norway. (*US Navy*)

economic resources of the region consisted of the minerals extracted from land areas – coal from Svalbard and cryolite from Greenland, for example – and the apparently inexhaustible fisheries stocks. Over the last ten years the increase in the price of oil and natural gas and the advances in the technology needed to extract them from deep waters prompted an extension of the search for offshore energy into the Northern Waters.

The lack of detailed international agreement on the division of the seabed only began to present problems when it was realised that the underground resources could be reached economically. Fishing, the major existing economic activity in these waters, had been seriously affected by more powerful catching techniques by the mid-1970s, when the littoral states

Hit and miss. The Cod War grew rougher and rougher as the Icelandic gunboats tried to cut the lines of British trawlers and Royal Navy escorts sought to fend them off. The Icelandic Coastguard patrol vessel *Thor* (right) falls astern of HMS *Andromeda* after suffering bow damage in a ramming attack on the British frigate. The gunboat *Odinn* (below) was luckier, escaping unscathed from this close shave with *Andromeda*. (*Royal Navy*)

Norwegian fast patrol boat *Rask* of the *Snogg* class. Norway and Denmark almost came to blows over fishing rights in 1981.

extended their sovereignty, in the form of exclusive fishery or economic zones, over what had previously been high seas. These new controls were imposed in order to conserve the fisheries and to increase the states' share of the fish caught off their coasts. However, the often uncertain demarcation of these zones, and their establishment before the United Nations Convention on the Law of the Sea had been drafted (let alone ratified), has led to conflict over the division of the Northern Waters' resources.

Iceland's extension of its fishing limits out to 12, 50 and then 200 miles, and the subsequent "Cod War" with the United Kingdom, could in the view of the North Atlantic Assembly have set the pattern for the whole region:

> "The 1973 Cod War between Iceland and the
> United Kingdom was an example of the kind of
> conflict that could arise over national resources
> and the possible consequences for stability and
> security in the North Atlantic."[4]

The declaration four years later of maritime zones in which one nation had exclusive access to resources could have led to new versions of the Cod War. Responding to the problems resulting from the Cod War, the European Community countries decided to extend their fisheries zones out to 200 miles from January 1, 1977. They were joined by a number of other Western countries that independently created various kinds of exclusive maritime zones. That conflict was largely avoided was partly due to a tacit agreement to use the continental shelf delimitation – where this already existed – for the division of

maritime zones. But agreement on the seabed boundaries had not been reached in much of the Northern Waters, and the creation of fisheries and economic zones produced a need for delimitation. Country ended up pitted against neighbouring country.

For a time in 1981 it seemed probable that Denmark and Norway would engage in a "Capelin War" around Jan Mayen; Greenland's maritime borders with its eastern neighbours – Iceland and Jan Mayen – have been the subject of delicate negotiations, claims and counter-claims; the Soviet Union and Norway dispute a vast area of continental shelf in the Barents Sea.[5] On the other hand, diplomacy has triumphed in many cases: the delimitation between Canada and Greenland in the Davis Straits, the seabed agreement between Iceland and Norway over Jan Mayen's southern zone,[6] and the annual Soviet-Norwegian accords over fishing in the "Grey Zone" off their northern coasts.[7]

Resource distribution and utilisation in Northern Waters has provoked tension or conflict between members of NATO (Britain and Iceland, for example), and between NATO and Warsaw Pact states, as witness the Soviet-Norwegian relationship in the Barents Sea. But it is in the matter of security that East-West rivalry is most obvious in these waters. The Northern Waters' strategic importance lies in their value as an avenue of commercial and military transit. The vulnerability of the West's transatlantic sea lanes to submarine attack, so painfully experienced in the Second World War, has been exacerbated by the creation of a large and capable Soviet submarine force. The area has seen an ever more obvious projection of Soviet naval surface and air power, drawn primarily from the vast reserves of the Northern Fleet, based so precariously in the Kola Peninsula.[8] This has been paralleled by NATO's creation of a surveillance and anti-submarine warfare barrier across the Greenland-

The spread of oil and gas production into the North Sea and beyond has left several of the NATO countries particularly vulnerable to Soviet economic warfare. Soviet Naval Aviation routinely overflies North Sea facilities: this is a Badger maritime reconnaissance bomber.

Iceland-United Kingdom (GIUK) gap. ICBMs travelling to and from the heartlands of the USA and USSR would overfly the region, as would strategic bombers. In response to this threat both sides have created surveillance and early-warning systems capable of observing aircraft and missile traffic throughout the region.

While much of the military activity in the Northern Waters relates to movement through them and precautionary measures to check it, the area contains a number of vital bases, those on the Kola Peninsula being the most obvious. The islands play a role in their own right, acting as platforms for the efforts to assist or frustrate transit through these waters. Military forces are however thin on the ground in Greenland, Jan Mayen, Iceland, the Faroes and Shetland, and no nuclear weapons are based on these islands in peacetime.[9] The Northern Waters have also acquired

Soviet Delta-class ballistic missile submarine.

Britain's response to the threat to its offshore resources includes both air and surface support. This Royal Navy Sea King (above) is shuttling a team of clearance divers between three gas production platforms following an anonymous warning that bombs had been planted on the rigs. Pictured passing one of the Humber gas platforms is the coastal minesweeper HMS *Soberton* (below). (*Royal Navy*)

an intrinsic strategic value as an arena for ballistic missile submarines and the hunter-killers that would pursue them. The increased range of the new SLBMs and SLCMs has made it possible to deploy the latest Soviet SSBNs – the Delta IV and Typhoon classes – further back in the Barents and Kola seas and under the Arctic ice cap, so reducing the need to transit through the potentially deadly North Norwegian and Greenland seas. In time of crisis or war Western naval forces would seek to penetrate the Barents Sea and carry out forward anti-submarine operations instead of trying to contain Soviet submarine forces at the GIUK gap. At all events, Soviet submarine commanders would be permitted no sanctuary in their own Arctic waters.[10]

This potential for conflict or increased tension has given rise to ideas of restraint at both government and private level. Could the superpowers, in the interests of peacetime political relations and strategic stability, arrive at mutual or unilateral controls on their employment of the Northern Waters as an arena of competition? Several existing agreements – such as the Incidents at Sea Agreement of 1972 – make a contribution but leave room for further efforts. A number of discussions have touched upon possible arms-control measures in the Northern Waters, including the creation of an Arctic nuclear weapon-free zone and the recognition of "sanctuaries" barred to anti-submarine forces.[11] Other possibilities include non-armament agreements, or more modest measures under which each side would confine itself to matching but not exceeding the other's exploitation of new technologies.[12]

The Northern Waters have witnessed a sometimes troubling interaction between economic and security issues. Western awareness of this relationship was reawakened by the rise in petroleum prices after 1973 and the accompanying realisation that supplies of strategic material were vulnerable to Soviet action or political chaos in the Third World. Since the late 1970s the United States has signalled a determination to maintain Western access to vital raw materials. Though the USA and USSR remain unlikely to lock horns over the raw materials to be found in the Northern Waters, economics and security do overlap there, in three different ways.

First, the Northern Waters flank the trade routes from North America to North-west Europe. The last world war showed that these routes must be protected if the Western European countries are to have any chance of surviving a period of crisis or blockade in the early stages of conflict. And in the event of a reinforcement operation, the convoys would pass through the same waters.

Second, there are resources within the Northern Waters region which are of great strategic value. Most important of these are the oil and gas reserves off the west coast of Norway, Northern Norway and the Shetland Islands. They have given rise to industrial activities in the Norwegian and British maritime zones which could be targets for attack. They also constitute a large proportion of Western Europe's petroleum reserves; as such they afford a measure of independence of Soviet and Middle Eastern sources. In the future, Greenland's uranium reserves could assume comparable significance.[13]

Third, nations in the area may be tempted to link their resources and security policies. This may be done to strengthen a bargaining position or to maximise gains in resource negotiations, and has occurred in the dealings between Norway and the Soviet Union in Svalbard and the Barents Sea, and during the disputes over fisheries limits between Britain and Iceland. In the Faroes and Greenland the US and NATO presence could be used as a bargaining counter in the debate over resource exploitation.[14]

Transportation of resources through the territorial sea, straits and exclusive economic zones of the Northern Waters could be affected by the new law of the sea. Plans for shipping lanes into the Arctic areas of Canada (through the Davis Straits) and into the northern shoreline of the Soviet Union (across the Arctic coast of Siberia) are both exciting and worrying. The challenge is to produce vessels that can economically use the traditional North-west and North-east passages. The danger is that this traffic may either fall foul of the extreme climate or pollute a fragile environment. Furthermore, neighbouring states have not always agreed about the conditions for Arctic transport; Greenland's complaints to Canada about the proposed Arctic Pilot Project are an example.[15]

New technology is also affecting military developments in the Northern Waters. While a number of these initiatives are primarily defensive – surveillance and anti-submarine warfare systems, for example – there have been some disturbing changes in offensive deployments. The advent of long-range air-launched and sea-launched cruise missiles increases the likelihood of the Northern Waters' becoming an arena for East-West conflict.[16] If in the near future the superpowers draw back from confrontation, the new détente could first show itself in the Northern Waters, in the form of reductions in armed strength and moves towards co-operation in scientific research and pollution control.

Whether the new significance recently attached to the Northern Waters leads to increased conflict in the area or to more co-operation will depend largely on the attitude of the countries involved. The governments of Canada, Denmark (and the home rule authorities in Greenland and the Faroes), Iceland, Norway and the United Kingdom (representing the Shetlands) have all shown a determination to take strong action to safeguard their resources and to protect the economic and security interests of their citizens. They have also shown a predilection for peaceful settlement of disputes – even the Cod War cost no lives – and for compromise. The main influences on peace and co-operation in the Northern Waters – the two superpowers – lie outside the area. It is their attitude towards security and resource-related questions which will finally determine whether the region remains calm or becomes more turbulent. The age of the Arctic may be upon us soon;[17] the day of the Northern Waters has already arrived.

The Island-class patrol boat HMS *Lindisfarne*, part of Britain's fishery protection fleet. (*Royal Navy*)

Impression of a Soviet *Norilsk*-class Arctic combi ship, fitted with an air-bubbling system designed to ease its passage through moderate ice. It is vessels like this that will make use of the North-east and North-west passages an economic proposition. (*Wartsila*)

Notes

1 This article is based on Chapter 1 in a forthcoming book edited by the authors – *Northern Waters: Resource and Security Issues* – to be published in September 1986 by Croom Helm for the Royal Institute of International Affairs.

2 See Louis Rey, "The Arctic Regions in the Light of Industrial Development: Basic Facts and Environmental Issues" in L. Rey (ed) *Arctic Energy Resources*; Elsevier, Amsterdam, 1983, pp 13–14.

3 These terms are used by Finn Sollie in a paper entitled *Arctic Development and its International Relevance*, presented at the International Symposium on the Sea, Tokyo, October 16–20, 1978.

4 North Atlantic Assembly Papers, *Security in the Northern Region*; The North Atlantic Assembly, Brussels, 1979, p 49.

5 See David Scrivener, "The Soviet Union and Northern Waters," in Archer and Scrivener (eds), as Note 1.

6 This question is dealt with by Robin Churchill, "Marine Delimitation in the Jan Mayen Area," *Marine Policy*, Vol 9, No 1, 1985, pp 16–38.

7 David Scrivener, "Soviet Policy on Legal and Resource Issues in the Barents Sea and Svalbard," *ASIDES* No 27; Centre for Defence Studies, Aberdeen, Spring 1986.

8 See "Soviet Naval Activities 1977–84," *NATO Review* No 1, 1985, pp 17–20.

9 Clive Archer, "Recent Developments in Nordic Security," *Contemporary Review* No 1420, Vol 244, May 1984, pp 243–8.

10 See chapters by Geoffrey Till, "Strategy in the Far North," and Steven Miller, "United States' Strategic Interests in Northern Waters," in Archer and Scrivener (eds), as Note 1.

11 These ideas are outlined in Hannah Newcombe, "A Nuclear-Weapon-Free Zone in the Arctic – A Proposal," *Bulletin of Peace Proposals*, Vol 12, No 3, 1981, pp 251–8, and Willy Ostreng, "Strategic Developments in the Norwegian and Polar Seas: Problems of Denuclearisation," *Bulletin of Peace Proposals*, Vol 13, No 2, 1982, pp 101–12.

12 Clive Archer and David Scrivener, "Nordic Security Issues," *ADIU Report*, Vol 5, No 4, July–August 1983, pp 4–6.

13 See Jorgen Taagholt, "Northern Waters: Resource Endowments," in D. Scrivener (ed), *Northern Waters – Resources and Security Issues. Papers and Proceedings of a Colloquium*; Centre for Defence Studies, Aberdeen, 1981, Ch 1.

14 See, for example, Clive Archer, "Greenland and the Atlantic Alliance," *Centrepiece* 7; Centre for Defence Studies, Aberdeen, Summer 1985, pp 22–39.

15 See Ole Heinrich (ed), *Arctic Pilot Project. Derfor er vi imod (APP: Why we are against it)*; Home Rule Information Service, Greenland, 1982.

16 See David Hobbs, "New Military Technologies and Northern Waters," in Archer and Scrivener (eds), as Note 1.

17 Oran Young, "The Age of the Arctic," *Foreign Policy*, Winter 1985, pp 160–179.

Navies in a terrorist world

Prof Paul Wilkinson

Small teams of very expert troops are a proven antidote to terrorist hostage-taking. Royal Marine Commando swimmers dive into action from an inflatable raiding craft.

Terrorism is not a synonym for violence and insurgency in general. It is a special kind of violence, a weapons system that can be used on its own or as part of a whole repertoire of unconventional warfare. In Central America, for example, terrorism is typically used with rural guerrilla and economic warfare in all-out bids to topple the government. But in Western Europe, which experiences about 40% of each year's international terrorist incidents, terrorism is usually unaccompanied by any wider insurgency. Wherever it occurs, terrorism takes the form of extreme and often indiscriminate violence directed against the innocent. Its typical tactics are bombings, shootings, assassinations, kidnapping, hijacking and other forms of hostage-taking for the purposes of extortion.

Terrorism can be defined as the systematic use of murder, injury, and destruction, or the threat thereof, to create a climate of terror, to publicise a cause, and to coerce a wider target into submitting to the terrorists' aims. This mode of violence becomes international when it is exported across frontiers or used against foreign targets in the terrorists' country of origin. While it is true that there are many campaigns in which terrorist violence is concentrated mainly in a single national territory or region (eg, the Basque region and Corsica), it is hard to find a pure case of domestic terrorism. By its very nature terrorism exploits the international environment, seeking support from and impact on foreign opinion and governments and making use of frontiers to obtain safe havens, arms supplies, more accessible or prestigious targets and, above all, greater exposure in the mass media.

Just as there is nothing new in the use of terrorism as a political weapon, so there is nothing novel about it being used afloat. Much of the activity of pirates down the ages amounted to the systematic terrorisation of civilian shipping and the taking of hostages for ransom. But in most cases these crimes were committed for the material enrichment of the pirates rather than for any political reason. By contrast, the great majority of modern terrorist acts are committed in support of explicit political or religio-political causes. The similarity between the two is that ruthless regimes of the kind that formerly indulged routinely in campaigns of piracy out of greed now frequently sponsor, support and utilise international terrorism as a tool of foreign policy.

A clear case of a state behaving in this way occurred at the very outset of the rise of contemporary terrorism, in January 1968. The *Pueblo*, a US Navy intelligence ship, was captured off the North Korean coast by a patrol boat from that nation. The US Government protested that the *Pueblo* had been in international waters at the time of its interception. However, in the course of the negotiations to obtain the release of the 82 surviving crewmen, the Americans were forced to make a "confession" and issue an "apology" for the ship's intrusion. Following the release of the crewmen on Christmas Eve 1968, the US publicly disavowed the confession and the apology.

Another early form of maritime warfare which tended to terrorise, whether by design or by its inevitable impact on the victims, was the practice of what the French call *guerre de course*, or commerce-destroying. The French perfected the technique against generally defenceless British merchant ships by deploying small, heavily armed vessels which would ambush their prey in the North Sea or the Channel and then scurry into the safety of their nearby ports. This was made all the easier when the Royal Navy was diverted from hunting down the cruisers and privateers by the task of watching the French Navy. There is no doubt that *guerre de course* could exact a heavy toll in suffering, injury and discontent from individual merchant ship owners and crews. One historian has estimated that between 1756 and 1760 alone the French privateers captured 2,500 English merchantmen. But the long-term strategic value of such operations is highly dubious, the growth of English merchant shipping at the time being so rapid that even losses on this scale did not seriously threaten the prosperity of the country as a whole.

An intensive campaign of commerce-destroying against the British merchant fleet today would have far more serious consequences, if only because of the dramatic decline in the size of the fleet. It has been estimated that Britain is losing merchant ships so fast that, at the present rate, we will have lost virtually all our major merchant vessels by 1994. Under these circumstances, and in the light of our continuing heavy dependence on sea transport for our survival as a trading nation, a protracted *guerre de course* or a major terrorist assault on our civilian shipping in ports and harbours would have deadly effect. This fact is unlikely to have escaped the attention of Admiral Gorshkov's disciples in Soviet Naval Command.

Just as the law applied to land warfare attempts to prohibit and punish crimes against humanity and war crimes, so, logically, should that governing the conduct of warfare at sea. Even if a comprehensive international code of this kind had been adopted by the majority of states, it would of course be very difficult to prevent wholesale breaches in the heat of war. But at least it would offer some framework of restraint. Unfortunately, international humanitarian law is exceptionally weak and inadequate in the maritime context. Those agreements which do exist date back to an earlier period of naval warfare and weaponry and are hedged around with all kinds of reservations. It is thus not surprising to find that in both world wars these crude and ambiguous rules tended to be more honoured in the breach than the observance.

P-4 torpedo boats like this one were used in the seizure of USS *Pueblo* by the North Korean Navy in 1968. (*US Navy*)

As its merchant fleet withers away, Britain becomes even more vulnerable to submarine interdiction of its seaborne trade. The tanker *British Forth* was available to be taken up from trade in support of the Falklands Task Force in 1982; by the mid-1990s the UK may have nothing like her. (*L. & L. van Ginderen*)

Nevertheless, the 1913 Oxford Manual contains some guidance on the laws covering naval operations which clearly anticipates and attempts to prevent terroristic use of violence at sea. For example, Article 12 of the draft code explicitly forbids privateering and ordains that "non-warships must not commit acts of hostility against the enemy". And in Article 15 methods of killing and injuring the enemy which involve treachery are forbidden. It is forbidden "to kill or wound an enemy who, having laid down his arms or having no longer means of defence, has surrendered at discretion" (Article 17 [1]), "to sink a ship which has surrendered before having taken off the crew" (Article 17 [2]), and "to declare that no quarter shall be given" (Article 17 [3]). Article 25 of the draft code prohibits "the bombardment of undefended ports, towns, villages, dwellings or buildings". And Article 20 forbids states to lay automatic contact mines, anchored or not, in the open sea.

What are the key trends? Is terrorism getting worse? By most calculations, the number of incidents of international and domestic terrorism combined is increasing at about 30% a year. Western democracies suffer the largest share of incidents, nearly 40% annually. Is international terrorism getting more lethal? In 1983 the United States lost more of its citizens through terrorist attacks in Lebanon alone than it had worldwide in the preceding 15 years. Suicide truck bombings, car bombs, time-delay fuzes

The United States lost more of its citizens to terrorism in the Lebanon in 1983 than it had in the whole world over the preceding 15 years. This Marine, on guard outside the US Embassy in West Beirut in 1984, stands behind a wire-mesh screen designed to detonate rocket-propelled grenades prematurely.

and other technological innovations have made terrorism potentially more destructive of life and property.

The resort of states to terrorism has grown markedly since 1980. Roughly 25% of each year's incidents can be linked to state sponsors, operating either directly or indirectly through funding, training, use of "diplomatic" facilities, weapons supply, and so on. The growing multiplicity of groups and causes vastly complicates the work of Western security authorities. Since autumn 1984 an additional and worrying headache has been the emergence of a self-styled international terrorist alliance of extreme leftist groups in Western Europe, aiming primarily at NATO. This includes the West German Red Army Fraction, the French Action Directe and the Belgian CCC. Leaders include Inge Viett, Nathalie Menigon and Jean-Marc Rouillan. These third-generation leftists are few in number but tough and cunning.

In Northern Ireland Britain faces Europe's severest terrorist problem. The result is the arming of the police as a matter of course – something that has never happened in mainland Britain – and a permanent British Army presence on the streets of the province.

They are difficult to catch, and have particularly much to gain by internationalising their attacks.

How serious is the security threat? Democracies are clearly vulnerable to terrorist attacks because of their openness and the ease of movement across and within their frontiers. It is always easy for extremists to exploit their freedoms with the aim of destroying democracy. But a well established democratic political system also has enormous inner strengths. By definition, the majority of the population see the government as legitimate and accountable. They willingly co-operate in the upholding of the law, and they rally against those who try to substitute the gun and the bomb for the ballot box. At no time in modern history has a European democracy been destroyed by a terrorist group and replaced by a pro-terrorist regime. Even so, it is clear that prolonged and intensive terrorism can be very damaging to the democratic governments and societies that experience it.

For example, in Northern Ireland and Spain terrorism not only fundamentally attacks innocent life and rights but also aims to undermine the democratic values, institutions, processes, and rule of law. By scaring away investment and disrupting industry and commerce, terrorism can gravely weaken the economy. At its most intensive, terrorist violence serves to incite hatred, promote and provoke intercommunal conflict and violence, and destroy the middle ground of normal politics. Unchecked, terrorism can easily escalate into civil war, which the terrorist may seek to exploit in order to establish a dictatorship.

In the long run, the threat to Western freedom from the spread of terrorism in the Third World is far more serious. For terrorism in these often highly unstable areas is much more likely to lead to the undermining of fragile democratic governments and is widely used as part of the repertoire of revolutionary movements to bring about Marxist takeovers. These wider revolutionary conflicts clearly alter the regional balance of power. They also threaten Western economic interests, such as access to oil and raw materials, and imperil lines of maritime communication at strategic chokepoints.

Internationally, terrorism is far more than a challenge to the rule of law and a clear threat to individual life and safety. For the United States, the major target of international terrorism all over the world, terrorism can be a major national security problem. For example, the handling of the seizure of the entire United States diplomatic mission in Tehran in 1979 became a colossal burden to the Carter Administration, hampering other activities and weakening US morale and prestige, particularly in the Middle East. More recently the bombing of US Marine barracks in the Lebanon not only took large numbers of lives but also severely curtailed President Reagan's military options in the Middle East and

Lebanese militiamen attack fellow Christians following attempts to end the civil war without seeking the sanction of President Amin Gemayel. The bewildering fragmentation and multiplicity of the opposing factions in the Lebanon makes countering terrorism there almost impossibly difficult for the intelligence services of the great powers.

authorities. Ironically, the *Maine* had been sent to Cuba to protect US citizens and property following the December 1897 riots in Havana.

In the First World War the German Government's obsessive pursuit of unrestricted submarine warfare, clearly designed to terrorise the neutral countries and the maritime community into abandoning sea links with Britain, led directly to the entry of the United States into the war. The most significant provocation to the US was the sinking of the 32,000-ton British liner *Lusitania* on May 7, 1915, by the submarine U-20. The ship was sailing from New York to Liverpool with a full complement of passengers, many of them Americans. She was torpedoed a few miles from the Irish coast and sank so swiftly that the lifeboats could not be properly loaded and lowered. Of the 1,959 passengers and crew, 1,198 were lost.

A more recent example of the grave consequences of maritime terrorism was the *Achille Lauro* affair. On October 8, 1985, Palestinian gunmen hijacked an Italian Mediterranean cruise liner, *Achille Lauro*, while she was off the coast of Egypt. The ship was carrying 511 passengers and crew, and the hijackers demanded the release of 50 Palestinian prisoners held in Israel. The Palestinians threatened to kill their hostages one by one – starting with the Americans – until their demands were met. After two days of zig-zagging around the eastern Mediterranean the hijackers were persuaded by fellow-Arabs to jump ship. It transpired that they had killed Leon Klinghoffer, an elderly American invalid confined to a wheelchair. This made the Americans all the more determined to bring the terrorists to justice, and when the Egyptians failed to extradite them US Navy F-14 Tomcat fighters from the carrier *Saratoga* were ordered to intercept the Boeing 737 which was flying the hijackers out of Egypt. The fighters caught the airliner 30 miles south of the Greek island of Crete at an altitude of about 34,000ft and with the 737 travelling at about 400mph. The position of the 737 had been pinpointed by Hawkeye AWACS aircraft. The Boeing was forced to land at Sigonella airbase in Sicily, where the hijackers were taken into custody by the Italian authorities. However, Palestinian Liberation Front leader Muhammed Abu Abbas, who was accompanying the hijackers and is believed by the US Government to have masterminded the ship hijack, was permitted by the Italians to go on his way. These events led to angry exchanges and a crisis in relations between the US and Egyptian governments; the toppling of Italian Prime Minister Craxi's government, which was bitterly divided over the handling of the affair; and a major setback to a Middle East peacemaking process involving King Hussein of Jordan, President Mubarak of Egypt, the Arafat wing of the Palestinian movement, and mediating Western European governments such as Britain's.

made it impossible for him to maintain a US presence, either through the multinational force or independently. The work of the suicide bombers deeply affected US opinion, Congress and the media, as it was clearly designed to do. Radical Palestinian groups such as Abu Nidal's Fatah Revolutionary Council may have been further emboldened by the apparent success of militant Shi'ite terrorism. There was growing circumstantial evidence by late 1985 that the Abu Nidal group was receiving valuable assistance from the secret services of several militantly anti-Western regimes, notably Libya, Iran and Syria. This loose international network constitutes a continuing threat to the security of the United States and its personnel and facilities not only in the Middle East but in the whole Mediterranean area and even further afield.

While it is true that at present terrorist attacks on shipping are relatively rare, the repercussions of such incidents are potentially far more serious for inter-national peace than those of typical terrorist attacks on land. For example, the destruction by an explosion of the US battleship *Maine* in Havana harbour in February 1898, leading to the death of 260 US seamen, contributed directly to the April 1898 US military intervention in the struggle between the Cuban independence movement and the Spanish colonial

The team that netted the men responsible for the *Achille Lauro* hijacking. E-2 Hawkeye early-warning and control aircraft (above) launched from the US Navy carrier *Saratoga* (inset) detected the Egyptian airliner in which the terrorists were being carried to safety. Then, under the close direction of a Hawkeye, a section F-14 Tomcats (one is seen below with an EA-6B Prowler in the background) intercepted the Egyptair Boeing 737 and forced it to land at Sigonella in Sicily. (*US Navy*)

Italian investigations of the hijacking and the murder of Mr Klinghoffer continue, and there are a number of theories as to the initial aims of the terrorists. PLF leader Abu Abbas has been widely reported as saying that the Palestinians did not intend to hijack the ship, and only did so when they were discovered cleaning their weapons. According to Abbas, the Palestinians' initial aim was to get to Ashdod, where they could carry out a suicide mission against Israel. Whatever the truth about the original plans of the terrorists, there is no doubt that the repercussions of the incident did nothing but harm to the Palestinian cause.

The hijack of *Achille Lauro* was by no means the first seizure of a ship by terrorists. For example, in January 1961 there was a dramatic take-over of a Portuguese liner off Venezuela by members of the Portuguese National Independence Movement. The ship's third officer was killed and another person wounded during the seizure. Following negotiations the passengers were allowed to disembark at Recife and Brazil gave asylum to the rebels. The ship was returned to its owners. In February 1974 a Greek freighter was hijacked in Karachi. The terrorists threatened to blow up the ship and kill the hostages unless the Greek authorities released two imprisoned Arab terrorists. The Greeks agreed to commute the sentences of the two and the hijackers were flown to Libya.

Yet although ship hijacking may appear all too easy in view of the laxity of shipboard and port security for civilian vessels, the fact is that it is a very rare occurrence. Less than a dozen ships have been hijacked in the last 20 years, and there has been nothing even vaguely resembling the plague of aircraft hijacks.

There are a number of reasons why ship hijacking has not caught on. It is far easier to attack targets ashore, while the impact upon the mass media is far greater on land. For those who seek more spectacular targets, there are still enough loopholes in airport security to make aircraft hijacking possible. If aviation becomes more difficult, terrorists will be driven to other forms of hostage-taking on land. Most terrorists are strictly landlubbers and have no taste for the storms and other rigours of the high seas. There are two other key tactical considerations which would deter the average small terrorist group. It is very difficult for a tiny group of hijackers to take and keep control of a major ship carrying a large crew and perhaps hundreds of passengers, all distributed among different decks and cabins. And it is in principle far easier for the authorities to mount a counterattack and regain control of the vessel. This is particularly the case now that a number of states have developed sophisticated anti-terrorist forces, such as Britain's Marine Commandos, which are expert in maritime counter-hijack techniques. The hijackers of *Achille Lauro* must have been well aware that if they had not jumped ship they would have been attacked by one of the formidable amphibious hostage-rescue forces in the area. The United States, Israel and Italy all had suitable forces ready to deploy.

By contrast, maritime zones such as ports and harbours, estuaries and navigable inland waterways

Royal Marines and Gurkhas aboard a rigid raiding craft of the kind that would be used for a fast run-in to an attack on a terrorist target.

provide an astonishingly varied array of high-value and easily accessible targets for the terrorist. By their very nature ports and harbours are extremely difficult to protect against terrorist bombers and gunmen. It is all too easy for terrorists to pass themselves off as tourists, passengers or dock workers and to gain access to vessels at the quayside. More sophisticated and better equipped groups can easily mount underwater operations against sitting targets. As was demonstrated by the sinking of the Greenpeace flagship *Rainbow Warrior* in Auckland Harbour by French agents, attacks of this kind have enormous psychological and symbolic effects. Although the secret agents who sank *Rainbow Warrior* were not part of a terrorist movement and certainly did not intend to kill anybody, there is no doubt that the enormous publicity given to the explosion, and the extensive international coverage of the shooting attack on a yacht in Larnaca Marina in 1985 in which three Israeli civilians were murdered, will have given terrorists a clear demonstration of the propaganda potential of maritime outrage.

Larger and more tactically sophisticated terrorist movements like the PLO saw the possibilities of attacks of this kind long ago. For example, in September 1978 Al Fatah planned to sail a freighter loaded with three tons of explosives into Israel's Sinai port of Eilat. They intended to fire 42 122mm rockets at the port's tank farm and then to run their boat on to the crowded beach. The plot was foiled by the Israeli Navy, which sank the freighter. Over the years the Palestinians have established a number of special units capable of maritime attacks on Israel, including attempts to fire anti-tank weapons and rockets at coastal targets. They have approached their objectives either aboard cargo vessels bound for Israel or in their own boats, launched from bases in Lebanon.

But it is not only the Palestinians who understand the rich potential of maritime terrorism against Western symbolic and economic targets. States which employ international terrorism as a routine weapon to undermine adversary nations and export revolution are also tempted by covert, easily denied, attacks on Western shipping and facilities in sensitive maritime zones such as EEZs or in strategic chokepoints. Western intelligence experts believe that Libya was responsible for a new and more deadly form of terrorist attack against shipping, using a commercial vessel to lay mines in the Red Sea in July 1984. A total of 18 merchant ships from various countries were damaged as a result.

There is clearly no reason why maritime targets should be immune from the general spread of international and domestic terrorism. While there are a number of practical considerations which deter, or at least greatly inhibit, terrorist activity against ships on the high seas and other offshore targets, these

The ill-fated *Greenpeace* is headed off in the South Pacific by the French frigate *Enseigne de Vaisseau Henry*.

The Israeli Navy is amply equipped with coastal patrol craft like this Dabur-class boat. They have gone into action a number of times against Palestinian seaborne raiding parties (*IAI*)

constraints do not apply to ships in harbour, ports or shore-based maritime facilities. Some states engaged in international terrorism can also deploy weapons which are normally found only in conventional warfare. Mining of a narrow seaway is one example of this type of campaign. We are likely to see SSMs and other more sophisticated ship-based weapons used in attacks mounted by rogue states or by their proxies.

Reaction to terrorism is just one of the many possible uses of limited naval force today. As James Cable points out in his *Gunboat Diplomacy*: "There have so far been relatively few examples of the marine variety (of terrorism), but it is not only the writers of thrillers who are concerned by the vulnerability of supertankers or by that barely defended bottleneck, the Straits of Hormuz. Even on land terrorists may be more accessible to aircraft launched from a carrier than to those compelled to overfly the territory of third parties."

If one examines the data on the 150 or so maritime terrorist incidents that have occurred worldwide, it becomes apparent that countermeasures must contend with a very wide range of activities. These include the smuggling of arms to terrorists by sea, the sinking of merchant ships, ship hijacks, sea-launched attacks on civilian population and property, and attacks on shore fuel storage facilities, shipyards, navy personnel and installations, and maritime offices.

Navies must use both offensive and defensive measures against this wide range of threats. Offensive measures could include raids on terrorist targets ashore, and attrition and disruption by means of such tactics as blockading and bombarding bases from the sea. Defensive naval operations would comprise satellite observation, airborne early-warning reconnaissance, radar surveillance, improvements to the defences of ships at sea, sea and air patrols to intercept arms supplies and raiding parties, and shore-based guards and patrols.

New early-warning systems and shipborne defensive weapons have greatly improved modern navies' capacity for local defence, giving them a significant superiority over their more primitively equipped terrorist adversaries. Detection methods are now so advanced that only a modern submarine has any real chance of making an unobserved approach to a ship at sea. Unfortunately, although terrorist movements do not normally possess submarines, terrorist states do and may use them to wage covert war.

Technological advances can however also be exploited by quite small terrorist groups for the purposes of counterattack. Navies need to be aware of the readiness with which fanatical groups can now obtain the techniques and resources to make remote-controlled bombs, together with a wide range of mortar, grenade and rocket launchers. NATO naval chiefs were surprised by the recent mortar attack on a squadron on the River Tagus, carried out by the extreme-left Portuguese terror group FP-25. Navies should also realise that they constitute a key target in the eyes of anti-NATO groups around Europe.

A more traditional yet still vital defensive maritime operation is the patrol to prevent the smuggling of arms and explosives to terrorists by sea. The Irish Navy had a spectacular early success of this type against the IRA on March 28, 1973, when it arrested the Cypriot coaster *Claudia* as she was trying to land a cargo of weapons on the Irish coast. The five tons of arms discovered included 250 Soviet-made rifles, mines, pistols, ammunition, grenades and explosives. Joe Cahill, a former commander of the Provisional IRA in Belfast, was on board. The ship was owned by a convicted West German arms smuggler, Gunther Leinhäuser, who said he had been given a shopping list of weapons by the IRA and that the arms had been provided by Colonel Gaddafi of Libya.

The first terrorist-inspired anti-ship missile attack cannot be long in coming. Though as yet no terrorist group disposes of the necessary means, there is no shortage of sympathetic governments with little regard for diplomatic niceties. This SSM-armed Nanuchka II-class fast attack craft is operated by the Libyan Navy.

There are many possible offensive uses of limited naval forces to combat terrorism. They can destroy bases in retaliation for attacks, rescue hostages, intercept and capture terrorists, enforce a punitive economic blockage, or make a show of force to back up political and diplomatic moves with an implied threat.

When the White House was considering America's response to last December's terrorist attacks at Rome and Vienna airports, practically all the military options reviewed would have involved the deployment of US naval forces. The Pentagon is known to have prepared a list of principal targets in Libya that could be hit in retaliation for Gaddafi's support for the Abu Nidal terrorists responsible for the airport outrages.

The Irish Navy scored one of the most notable recent successes against terrorism, arresting the Cypriot coaster *Claudia* in the Eastern Atlantic as she tried to run a cargo of IRA arms into the west coast of Ireland. This is the P21-class patrol vessel *Emer*.

The US Navy carrier *Coral Sea*, currently deployed in the Mediterranean in an effort to dissuade Libya's Colonel Gadaffi from lending further support to the Middle Eastern groups who have been directing their attacks at US citizens around the world. (*US Navy*)

The British royal yacht *Britannia* proved very useful during operations to rescue civilians caught up in the recent fighting in South Yemen. (*Royal Navy*)

When the US carrier *Coral Sea* was ordered to sail from Naples, some jumped to the conclusion that the aircraft aboard would be used to carry out air strikes against Libya. In reality the US Government knew that the scope for military action was almost negligible. Such measures would have put the lives of the 1,500 Americans still in Libya and the thousands of other expatriates from Western countries immediately at risk. Furthermore, in view of the sizeable presence of Russian military advisers and other personnel in Libya, any attack could easily have escalated to a general war in the Mediterranean and even beyond. These are the basic reasons why economic, political and diplomatic sanctions to isolate Gaddafi became the US Administration's preferred policy. It is sad that the Western European allies failed to see the possibilities of combined action against Libya and preferred to put their short-term commercial interest in Libyan trade before the protection of innocent civilians against international terrorism.

One of the key lessons of the Falklands War was that a nation with far-flung vulnerabilities and responsibilities cannot afford to be without adequate and flexible forces, including carrierborne air power, capable of responding to out-of-area contingencies.

The recent brilliant rescue operation by *Britannia* in South Yemen underlines this. But to counter terrorism, the appropriate mix of ships and seaborne air power is not enough. There must also be adequate training in the nature of the threat and in the proven techniques and tactics for combating it. Until very recently few Western navies bothered to pay any attention whatsoever to this problem. But terrorism has now become the characteristic mode of violent conflict, and it should at least be included in naval staff college programmes and accorded an appropriate place in naval planning and exercises.

Another important lesson of the Falklands War, and one which applies equally to the fight against terrorism, is the key role of special forces such as the Special Boat Squadron (SBS) and the Special Air Squadron (SAS). The US has some good units with a special amphibious assault capability (such as the SEALs), but they are far too small in numbers and are gravely in need of additional resources for training and equipment.

But it is not just regular naval forces that must adapt to meet the terrorist threat. Civilian crews and the staff who work in ports and harbours are notoriously lax in matters of security. They must adjust to the fact that they are increasingly likely to be affected by terrorism. The civilian maritime industry must also urgently review its training, contingency planning and general preparedness. As all good naval commanders know, the art of self-defence lies in identifying your weakest points and doing your best to rectify them.